# Access Essentials
# 2019

## M.L. HUMPHREY

# SELECT TITLES BY M.L. HUMPHREY

## ACCESS ESSENTIALS 2019

Access 2019 Beginner

Access 2019 Intermediate

## EXCEL ESSENTIALS 2019

Excel 2019 Beginner

Excel 2019 Intermediate

Excel 2019 Formulas & Functions

Excel 2019 Formulas and Functions Study Guide

## WORD ESSENTIALS 2019

Word 2019 Beginner

Word 2019 Intermediate

## POWERPOINT ESSENTIALS 2019

PowerPoint 2019 Beginner

PowerPoint 2019 Intermediate

# CONTENTS

# Access 2019 Beginner

ACCESS ESSENTIALS 2019 BOOK 1

M.L. HUMPHREY

# CONTENTS

# CONTENTS (CONT.)

# Introduction

Microsoft Access is vital to helping me run my business. As a small business owner in a rapidly evolving industry there aren't a lot of off-the-shelf tools that I can use to analyze my sales of my products across varying platforms. And even when there are tools that exist they rarely keep up with the pace of change.

For example, I may add a new sales platform today but that vendor with that fancy sales program may not be able to include it in their reporting for six months. Since my ability to pay my rent relies on my knowing what products of mine sell where and whether they're actually making me a profit, I can't afford to wait for someone else to play catch-up.

That's why I rely on Microsoft Access. Because it allows me to build a customized reporting system that combines sales of multiple products in multiple formats across multiple sales platforms. And to generate any report I need in real-time. It may take a few hours to build that report, but I know I can do that and have the information I need immediately.

(I have also in the past used Access on consulting projects where we needed to track large amounts of text. Excel has its limitations in terms of how much it will actually display in a cell without manual resizing the row height and Word is a little too static for some purposes, so Access becomes the best choice in those scenarios.)

Now, to be clear, my approach to Access is not the old-school approach to Access. Back in the day Access was great for keeping a customer contact database, for example. Or I think some people even used it as a sales-tracking database. But technology has evolved to the point where using Access in those ways doesn't really make sense. There are plenty of off-the-shelf customer database and accounting programs that are much better structured for end-users than Access is.

If you want that kind of approach, this is probably not going to be the book for you. This book is for those who know how to use Microsoft Excel but need just that little bit more than Excel can offer. My focus is on bringing in outside data and linking it to generate summary reports and analysis.

Also, if you're at a larger company, talk to your IT department before you use Access. First, you might be surprised what they already have available in-house and second, a lot of IT departments are not exactly thrilled to have rogue Access databases that they don't know about. These tend to pop up in a department that's just going to track one little thing without bothering IT and then suddenly five years later that database is crucial to operations and doesn't have the appropriate controls built around it and everyone gets very upset.

One more thing to consider before we get started. I think Access has a valuable role for small companies, but at some point if you get large enough or are dealing with significant enough amounts of data it's quite possible you will outgrow Access. When that happens, you need to start looking towards programs like R and hiring computer programmers and people who throw around words like big data.

(I'm not a computer programmer so don't take my word on that. Just understand that when you get big enough and complicated enough you need to move to more sophisticated solutions.)

Alright. Now that we have that all out of the way, what will this book actually cover with respect to Access?

I am going to walk you through how Access databases work, the four main components of Access, the key differences I see between working in Access and Excel, and then how to complete basic tasks in Access as well as navigate through the various parts of Access.

Once we have that foundation established, we'll discuss the two ways to create tables, how to export an existing Access data table or query to Excel, how to add data to a table from an external Excel file, the most common field data types, table views, and how to amend data in a table.

We'll then discuss how to perform various tasks in tables and queries, such as selecting records or columns and changing row heights or column widths.

From there we'll cover select queries including how to create a basic detail query and how to create a basic summary query using only one table or query as the source. This will be done using the Query Wizard. We'll also cover the types of query views available and the Design View in particular.

Next we'll discuss table relationships and how to use them to create detail and summary queries that use more than one table or query as their source. And we'll discuss how to use basic criteria to narrow down the results in a query.

Finally, we'll cover summary results, sorting data, and filtering data in tables and queries. And then we'll finish with a brief discussion about forms, reports, and printing.

By the time you're done with this book you should be able to comfortably navigate Access and work with tables and queries at a beginner level.

There is a companion to this book called *Access 2019 Intermediate* that continues from that point to cover how to customize forms and reports and how to create union or crosstab queries. But when you're done with *Access 2019 Beginner* you should have enough knowledge to be able to take multiple Excel and .csv files and combine them to create your own summary reporting. *Access 2019 Intermediate* just adds another level of sophistication to what you create and covers some of the more esoteric options that you won't necessarily need on a regular basis.

Before we dive in on all of that I will walk through opening and saving and deleting files in Access which will seem very simplistic if you've ever worked in another Microsoft Office program (which I hope you have). But it's important to walk through because there are little differences that you need to understand.

Finally, this book is written using Access 2019. All of the screenshots and how-to steps will be written from that perspective.

If you have an earlier version of Access, the books *Access for Beginners* and *Intermediate Access* were written using Access 2013 and with a more generalized approach that should work for any version of Access from 2007 onward.

There are some fiddly little differences between the different versions of Access, but the concepts, general location of options, and the approach remain the same across versions.

Alrighty then. Now that you know what we're looking to accomplish, let's start with some basic terminology.

# Basic Terminology

To make sure that we're on the same page, I'm going to start with some basic terminology. Some of this will be standard to anyone talking about Access and some of it is my personal quirky way of saying things, so best to skim through if nothing else.

## Tab

I refer to the menu choices at the top of the screen (File, Home, Create, External Data, Database Tools, Help, etc.) as tabs. If you click on one you'll see that the way it's highlighted sort of looks like an old-time filing system.

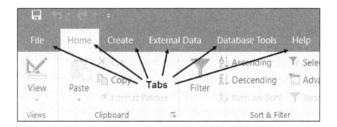

Each tab you select will show you different options. For example, in the image above, I have the Home tab selected and you can do various tasks such as change views, cut/copy/paste, sort and filter, refresh your data, add/save/delete a record, add a totals row, check spelling, and more. Other tabs give other options.

# Click

If I tell you to click on something, that means to use your mouse (or trackpad) to move the cursor over to a specific location and left-click or right-click on the option. (See the next definition for the difference between left-click and right-click).

If you left-click, this selects the item. If you right-click, this generally creates a dropdown list of options to choose from. If I don't tell you which to do, left- or right-click, then left-click.

# Left-Click/Right-Click

If you look at your mouse or your trackpad, you generally have two flat buttons to press. One is on the left side, one is on the right. If I say left-click that means to press down on the button on the left. If I say right-click that means press down on the button on the right.

Not all trackpads have the left- and right-hand buttons. In that case, you'll basically want to press on either the bottom left-hand side of the trackpad or the bottom right-hand side of the trackpad.

# Dropdown Menu

If you right-click on something in Access, for example a field or table name, you will generally see what I'm going to refer to as a dropdown menu. (Sometimes it will actually drop upward if you're towards the bottom of the screen.)

A dropdown menu provides you a list of choices to select from like this one that you'll see if you right-click on a field in a new table:

There are also dropdown menus available for some of the options listed under the tabs at the top of the screen. For example, if you go to the Home tab, you'll see small arrows below or next to some of the options, like the View option and the Refresh All option on the Home tab. Clicking on those arrows will give you a dropdown menu with a list of additional choices.

## Expansion Arrows

I don't know the official word for these, but you'll notice at the bottom right corner of most of the sections in each tab that there are also arrows. If you click on one of those arrows Access will bring up a more detailed set of options, usually through a dialogue box (which we'll discuss next) or by adding a task pane (which we'll define after that).

In the Home tab, for example, there are expansion arrows for Clipboard and Text Formatting. Holding your mouse over the arrow will give a brief description of what clicking on the expansion arrow will do like here for the Clipboard section on the Home tab:

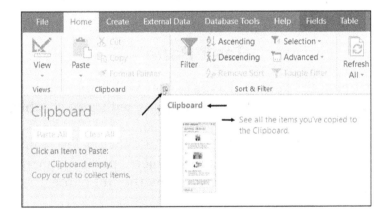

## Dialogue Box

Dialogue boxes are pop-up boxes that cover specialized settings. As just mentioned, if you click on an expansion arrow, it will often open a dialogue box that contains more choices than are visible in that section. When you click on the expansion arrow for the Text Formatting section of the Home tab, for example, that brings up the Datasheet Formatting dialogue box which looks like this:

While Access does have some dialogue boxes, they aren't near as common as in Excel.

# Task Pane

When you first open an Access database you will notice that there is a main workspace on the right-hand side, which opens with a new table, Table1. This takes up most of the screen.

On the left-hand side of that table, however, is what I'm going to refer to as a task pane. In this case it's the All Access Objects pane. You can see the title at the top. Here I've expanded it enough to show the full name.

A task pane is a separate section that contains information or options aside from what you see in the main workspace. (Panes often show up in PowerPoint as well.)

The All Access Objects pane is where you go to easily navigate between your tables, queries, forms, and reports. It can be minimized but not closed.

Other panes can be opened and closed as needed and will appear on either the left-hand side or the right-hand side of the main workspace depending on the pane.

To see an example of one that can be closed, click on the expansion arrow in the Clipboard section of the Home tab to open the Clipboard pane. It should open on the left side of the All Access Objects pane.

To close a pane like the Clipboard pane which can be closed, click on the X in the top right corner.

If instead of an X there is a double-arrow in the top right corner (like with the All Access Objects pane as you can see above) you can click on the double arrow to minimize the pane. If a pane has already been minimized there should be a double arrow in the same top section that you can click on to expand it once more.

(The pane I refer to as the All Access Objects pane because that's how it's labeled at the top is shown as the Navigation Pane when minimized.)

To change the width of a pane, hold your mouse over the inner edge of the pane until you see a double-sided arrow pointing left and right, left-click, and drag until the pane is your desired width.

## Scroll Bar

Scroll bars allow you to see your data when there is sufficient data to take up more space than is currently available on the screen.

When you have enough tables, queries, reports, and forms, there will also be a scroll bar visible on the right-hand side of the All Access Objects pane.

In the image above there is a scroll bar along the bottom of the data table.

To move through your data using the scroll bar, you can left-click on the bar itself and then hold the left-click as you drag the bar. You should see a change to what's visible in your task pane or your data table as you do so. How fast that change occurs depends on how fast your drag the scroll bar.

Or you can click in the gray area to either side of the scroll bar to move in that direction approximately one screen at a time.

You can also click on the arrows visible at the ends of the scroll area to move approximately one row or one column at a time.

## Arrow

If I ever tell you to arrow to the left or right or up or down, that just means use your arrow keys. If you're clicked onto a cell in your table this will usually move you one cell in the direction of the arrow you used. However, if you are double-clicked into a cell so that you can edit the text, arrowing right or left will move you to the right or left one character space within the cell.

## Tab Through or Tab To

I may instead tell you to tab through or tab to your data. This is different from the tabs we discussed above. In this instance, we're talking about using the Tab key. If you are in a cell and you use the Tab key it will move you to the right one cell. If it's the end of the row it will move you to the first cell of the next row.

Using the Shift key and the Tab key together will move you to the left one cell. If you're at the beginning of a row it will move you to the end of the row just above.

(Using the Tab key is a handy way to highlight an entire cell if you need to copy the value for some reason. Click on a cell to either side, Tab or Shift + Tab to get into the cell you want, and then copy using Ctrl + C.)

## Cursor

There are two possible meanings for cursor. When you're clicked into a cell in a data table, you will see that there is a blinking line which is the cursor. This version of the cursor indicates where you are in the cell.

If you type text, each letter will appear where the cursor was at the time you typed it. The cursor will move (at least in the U.S. and I'd assume most European versions) to the right as you type. This version of the cursor should be visible at all times when you're working in a data table.

The other type of cursor is the one that's tied to the movement of your mouse or trackpad. If this cursor is positioned over your data, it will usually look somewhat like a tall skinny capital I. If you move it up to the menu options or off to the sides, it becomes a white arrow. (Except for when you position it over any option under the tabs that can be typed in such as font size or font where it will once again look like a skinny capital I.)

It can also look like a small squat cross or a double-sided arrow at times depending on what you're able to do at that moment.

Usually I won't refer to your cursor, I'll just say, "click" or "select" or whatever action you need to take with the cursor. Moving the cursor to that location will be implied.

# Table

There are actually two different types of tables I talk about in Access.

Later when we discuss the four main components of an Access database, one of those will be Tables. In that meaning, tables are data tables where your imported or input data is stored.

But if you look at a query in Datasheet View, this too is what I would describe as a table of data because the information is stored in columns and rows like you would see in an Excel worksheet.

# Column/Field

Every data table in Access consists of rows and columns of information. Columns, which can also be referred to as fields, run across the top of the workspace and are named Field1, Field2, etc. by default. The name of each column/field can be changed to a user-provided name.

In the image below, the columns/fields in this table are ID, Month, Year, and Field3 .

| ID | MonthOfSale | YearOfSale | Field3 | Click to Add |
|---|---|---|---|---|
| 1 | January | 2020 | | |
| 2 | February | 2020 | | |
| 3 | March | 2020 | | |
| 4 | April | 2020 | | |
| 5 | May | 2020 | | |
| 6 | June | 2020 | | |
| * | (New) | | | |

# Row/Record

Rows/records run downward in a data table.

The table pictured above has six rows/records in it. In that case there is an ID field and those records are numbered sequentially. But they don't have to be.

In the below image we have a table with four records in it. Note that the records with an ID of 1 and 4 have been deleted so there is no longer a record with either of those ID numbers in the table. Even if you were to add a record with the same information into it back into the table, you could not have a Record 1 or 4 in that table because those records were deleted from the table.

| ID | MonthOfSale | YearOfSale | Field3 | Click to Add |
|----|-------------|------------|--------|--------------|
| 2 | February | 2020 | | |
| 6 | June | 2020 | | |
| 3 | March | 2020 | | |
| 5 | May | 2020 | | |
| (New) | | | | |

Also, as you can see above, records do not have to be listed in sequential order. If there is an ID number in a table that ID number will be tied to the record in that particular row so that if you change the sort order of your data the ID number moves with its record. This is different from how Excel works where the row number is tied to the row and exists for ease of reference.

So while a data table in Access can look much like a worksheet in Excel, it works very differently. Think of each row of a data table in Access as containing a related set of information that will always stay together. Technically, this is best referred to as a record. However, because I approach Access as an Excel user, I may still sometimes refer to rows of data.

The ID column is optional, so if you think that having it in your table will create confusion or difficulty, you don't have to use it.

## Cell or Entry or Value

When I refer to a cell in Access I am referring to the intersection of a column and row. In the Columns screenshot above the Year associated with the record with ID 4 is 2013. That value, 2013, is stored in a cell.

Cell is once more terminology that I bring over from using Excel.

It is probably more appropriate to refer to values or entries but in a generic sense I will still say something like, "click into the cell next to the cell that contains the value you want to copy."

## Control Shortcuts

In Access there are various control shortcuts that you can use to perform tasks like save, copy, cut, and paste. I don't use control shortcuts near as much in Access as I do in Excel or Word, but they are available.

Each time I refer to one it will be written as Ctrl + a capital letter, but when you use the shortcut on your computer you don't need to use the capitalized version of the letter.

For example, holding down the Ctrl key and the c key at the same time will copy any highlighted entry. I'll write this as Ctrl + C, but that just means hold down the key that says Ctrl and the c key at the same time.

# Undo

Access does have an Undo option which will generally let you undo your last action. It's available in the Quick Access Toolbar in the top left corner of the screen or by using Ctrl + Z.

However, Undo is not nearly as powerful in Access as it is in Excel or in Word and you should not rely on it. Sometimes it doesn't work at all. Or it undoes one type of action while you were hoping it would undo another. Or only undoes one record change when you need to undo ten

So be very careful with your entries and be sure to save a copy of your database before you start doing anything that might break it or change large amounts of your data, because in Access you will not be able to get that information back or reverse those changes the way you would be able to in Excel.

# How An Access Database Works

Alright, now that we've covered basic terminology, we need to take a crash course in how databases work and why you use them.

At its most basic, a database stores information and organizes that information for easy search and retrieval. Technically an Excel worksheet is a database. It's called a flat file database. Everything is stored in one set of rows and columns in a single table.

What Access lets you do is create what's called a relational database where you can take multiple tables of data and relate them to one another to create more complex reports. Access is what's referred to as a database management system (DBMS).

There are two main reasons, in my opinion, to work with relational databases.

One, it allows you to keep from repeating the same information over and over and over again. This saves potential data entry errors as well as takes up less space, which can be important when dealing with a large set of data.

So rather than have customer first name, customer last name, street address, city, state, and zip code followed by transaction amount and transaction date for every single transaction a company does, you can store in one location one time the customer information and then link that to a unique Customer ID which you then use in a second location where you store transaction information.

Because you have the Customer ID in both locations, you can pull in that customer information at any time without having to repeat it and store it for every single customer transaction. This can be a significant savings in terms of space used and computation time.

Let's quickly walk through an example to see what I mean by that:

Assume there are six pieces of information we've collected on a customer (first name, last name, street address, city, state, and zip code). For every transaction we also collect transaction date and amount. That's eight pieces of information per transaction.

If we had five transactions for Customer Jones that's forty pieces of information we'd need to store using a flat file database.

However, in a relational database, like Access, you can take the six pieces of customer information and associate them with one Customer ID. And then for each transaction you'd only need Customer ID, transaction amount, and transaction date.

That means we only have to store twenty-two pieces of information (three times five plus seven) instead of forty. That's just a little over half as much information as before and that's only for one customer and five transactions.

Multiply that times thousands of customers and thousands of transactions and you can begin to see how powerful using a relational database can be, especially if you're trying to perform calculations on that data.

(Although as discussed in the introduction, when you reach the point where this really starts to matter, I think Access is probably no longer the best solution and you probably shouldn't be doing the work on your own.)

The second use for a relational database, and why I use Access the most, is that it allows you to take data from multiple sources and tie them together to create summaries of that information.

So, for example, let's say I have sales reports from three different vendors for twenty different books. Each of those vendors gives me sales reports with different columns of information and with different identification numbers for each book.

Vendor A labels my first book AEFG345. Vendor B labels it 123578. Vendor C labels it H2T45.

Ideally they would all use the same title that I gave them, but they don't. Sometimes they add the subtitle, and one vendor adds the library name to the title every single time a book sells to a library.

This means I can't just copy and paste the title, units sold, and amount earned from those three vendor reports into an Excel worksheet and create a pivot table to see total sales.

Because without doing something to tie those records together, I have nothing to effectively link the data across those three reports. The identifiers are different and the titles are different.

What I can do, though, is put those three vendor reports into Access and add one more table where I tell Access that for Title A the identifier is AEFG345 at

Vendor A, 123578 at Vendor B, and H2T45 at Vendor C. I can then build a query to pull the sales information for that title from all three reports.

The key with a relational database is that the different tables of data need to link to one another somehow. They need to have a relationship.

And you need to tell Access what that relationship is. Your whole relational database is based upon, no surprise here, relationships between your different data tables.

In the customer transaction example I walked through above, we had Customer ID to link the customer information table to the customer transaction table.

That is the traditional way of working with a relational database. You have a customer information table with Customer ID. You have a product table with Product ID. You have a branch office table with Branch ID. You have a Sales Representative or Employee table with Sales Representative ID or Employee ID. And then you have a table with more granular transaction information that leverages all of those IDs.

So you might list transaction date, Customer ID, Product ID, Sales Rep ID, and sales amount for a transaction. Transaction date and sales amount are unique to that transaction. The rest can be referred to using the ID numbers and those other tables of data.

Basically what happens is that you're taking one big set of data and extracting the bits that repeat themselves and then replacing them with an identifier.

That is the traditional way that people use relational databases.

The way I use a relational database is a bit backwards from that.

As I mentioned above, I take unrelated reports—the reports from each of my vendors—and build a master table that tells Access how to relate them to one another. Think of the master table I use as a decoder key. It says that for Product A when we're looking at Table 1, this is how it's identified. When we're looking at Table 2, this other way is how it's identified. And in Table 3, it's this third way.

Using a master table like that lets me go to each separate vendor and pull in the information for that product no matter how that vendor has chosen to identify that product or what order they've chosen to provide their information in.

Even though my approach is vastly different from the standard approach, at heart both approaches are still based on relationships. For either approach to work, you must have unique identifiers in each table that you can link to.

You can't have 123 be the Customer ID for both Customer Jones and Customer Smith in the same data table. 123 must be the Customer ID for one unique customer in that data table and that cannot be changed or reused.

Also, when you're building your database, you have to make sure that there is something in each table of data that can be linked to your other tables of data, and that the value you choose to link on is unique to that product, customer, etc. within that data table.

We'll walk through this more later, so if it sounds confusing right now, don't worry.

The basic message to take away here is that Access works by taking different tables of data and linking them to one another so that you can then create queries that pull that information together into one central location when needed.

# Four Main Components Of An Access Database

Okay. Now that you have the basic idea of what we're trying to do by using Access which is to upload various tables of information and then link them so we can create queries based on what's in more than one of those tables, let's walk through the four main components of an Access database.

(As determined by me based on the way Access is organized.)

Those components are Tables, Queries, Forms, and Reports.

Each one that you create within your Access database will be shown by default in its own section in your All Access Objects pane. Like so:

## Tables

Tables are the bedrock upon which everything else is built. As a matter of fact, everything else would be blank without your data tables because the other three components only store a way to pull or display the data that's kept in your tables. Each time you generate a query, report, or form, it uses the information in your tables to build that query, report, or form.

Delete your tables and your queries, forms, and reports will be blank.

That's why tables are listed at the top. This is your raw data. This is the primary place where you input, edit, and delete the information used in your database.

Each table should be unique in terms of what it contains. You shouldn't need to have multiple tables with the same information in them.

In my database I have a table of sales information for each vendor as well as my master title table that links it all together.

In a more traditional database there might be customer, product, employee, transaction, and sales tax data tables.

It is up to the user(s) of the Access database to define what columns of data are in each table and to provide the values that go into each record.

You can create tables manually in Access where you directly input information.

Or you can do what I do for the most part which is upload data to Access to either create a table or add new records to an existing table.

(Don't worry, we'll walk through how to do both options later and then you can decide what works for you. The key right now is that tables are what everything else depends on and where your data is stored.)

# Queries

Queries are where you tell Access how to pull together the information in your various data tables or from other queries.

If you think of your data tables as a big juicy buffet of food, then a query is the equivalent of going through that buffet and loading up a plate with just the items you want. You take a little bit of customer information from here, a little bit of product information from there, add in some cost data and sales data, and now you have a query that shows you profit and loss by product and customer.

Queries are where the bulk of the analysis is done. Your tables are the raw material, your queries are where you put that material together to make something useful.

I have far more queries than tables. When I was preparing to write *Access for Beginners* I counted and I had twenty-two tables of data and one hundred and ten queries. At this point I'm sure I have upwards of a hundred and fifty queries because I have year-specific queries in my database. (Queries built to pull in 2020 data or 2021 data.)

Before you panic, understand that the queries you use will grow organically over time. You very likely will not sit down on day one and create a hundred-plus queries. You'll probably start with a small handful that will grow as you decide you want to sample your data in different ways.

So. Queries are where you pick and choose the information you want and combine it together to perform the calculations and analysis that you need.

# Forms

Forms are something I have used for corporate clients in the past, but that I don't tend to use for my own Access database. A form displays each record from a table in a more user-friendly way. It's like if someone took all that data you input and printed it on a letter-size piece of paper with nice formatting.

Forms are very useful for when you want to input data directly into your Access database. So, for example, if you had a customer contact database that you had created in Access, it would likely be easier to input a new customer using a form instead of a table.

Forms are especially useful when you're dealing with entries that contain a large amount of text because it is far easier to type in text when there's a big text field than in a small cell in a data table.

Access will easily take a data table and create a form for you. For example, this is a form for the data table we looked at earlier that had two main fields, MonthOfSale and YearOfSale.

And once your data is in a form you can edit the values in that form and it will update your data table as well. (Except the identifier field which is set up to be a non-changeable value that identifies the record.) Which again is great if you're doing direct data input in your Access database and dealing with lengthy entries.

BUT.

Both in data tables and in forms you need to be very careful if you're editing or inputting information in Access. Because any change you make will be saved the minute you make that change. You can't type in ten entries, realize you were making a mistake, and close out the form without those changes being saved. Which is why I prefer to do the majority of my fiddling with my data in Excel and then upload it to Access for analysis and display only.

As I've mentioned before there are probably better commercially-available options out there if what you need is to collect information from your users through some sort of interface. But that's why forms are there in Access.

# Reports

Reports are just what they sound like, reports. They take the information you have in a table or query and they put it in a report format that has better formatting for print or distribution.

In a report you can change the font or font size, add section headers and footers, add subtotals by section, only include certain fields, arrange how the fields appear on the page, and much more.

A report can pull from multiple sources, but I tend to use methods for generating reports that require that all of the information be in a single query or table already.

\* \* \*

So those are your four basic components of an Access database. As I mentioned in the introduction, this book is going to focus on creating tables and basic queries because I think that's the foundational knowledge you need to use Access.

At the very end we will cover how to generate a basic report or form, but not how to customize either one. That's covered in *Access 2019 Intermediate*.

Okay. Now that you know the four main components of an Access database, let's discuss the key differences between Access and Excel that make working in Access far more dangerous than working in Excel.

# Access Versus Excel And The Dangers Of Working In A Database Environment

One of my favorite things to say when talking about Excel is that Ctrl + Z, Undo, is your friend. In Excel if you write a formula wrong or delete the wrong data or sort wrong or filter wrong, you just Ctrl + Z until you're back to where you were before.

That is not the case with Access.

Let me repeat but in a slightly different way.

Access does have an Undo option, but it is extremely limited. A lot of times it will undo exactly one thing and one thing only. So if you edit one thousand records at once, it will undo one of those edits. Also, it doesn't undo everything. Sometimes you do something in Access, realize you made a mistake, and there's no going back.

That's because Access is at heart a database application. It is meant to store data and then to allow you to use that data for reports and calculations. The nature of a database like that is that you change a record and the change sticks. There is no, "Well, I didn't save so I can just close it and we'll be fine" with Access.

Oh no.

The minute you delete a value and move on to a new record, that value is gone. You can't get it back. If you overwrite a value and move on, that value is overwritten. If you put in a garbage entry in Access, that value is saved. As soon as you make a change to a record in a table and move on, that change sticks. This includes if you make a change to a table through a query or a form.

(For formatting or design changes, Access will ask if you want to save them. But not data changes.)

This is why I prefer to store my raw data outside of Access and do any adjustments or analysis on that data in a different file, usually Excel.

It's also why I am not a fan of direct data entry in Access, because there's no backup if you get it wrong. Not unless you enter your information and then export it and store it outside of Access.

The other reason I prefer to work in Excel first is because Access views every single record in a data table as its own standalone record.

What that means practically speaking is that you can't copy and paste a value down an entire column easily the way you can in Excel.

For example, if I want to enter "Mystery" in a hundred rows in Excel I can type it once, copy it, and paste it down the next 99 rows. I'm done in ten seconds. In Access, it doesn't work that way. You'd have to copy the entry and then paste it into each of those 99 records one by one.

In Excel I can also go to the next row, start to type "m" and as long as there are no other entries that start with an m, Excel will suggest "mystery" for my value. Again, that doesn't happen in Access because each record is treated separately.

So while the data tables in Access and Excel look a lot alike, they do not behave alike.

You may be thinking to yourself, when would this even come into play?

Well, let me give you an example.

I get vendor reports that I upload to Access on a monthly basis. And I like to know my sales by month for each product. But most of the vendor reports I receive only use a date. Or, worse, they use a date range which sometimes crosses months which makes it almost impossible to pull out the month of the transaction using a formula.

But since I know what month that report pertains to when I upload it, I just add two additional columns—month and year—to my Excel spreadsheet before I upload. That lets me easily pull a report of sales by month/year for every product on every vendor.

In Excel I can add those columns in less than a minute. I add the values into the first row, highlight those entries, double-click in the bottom right corner to copy to the rest of the rows, change the setting so that it's a copy of those values and not a series, and I'm done.

In Access? Not so easy.

Imagine I have a thousand records where I have to add a month and year. I can't set up a rule because next month it'll be a different month and maybe a different year, so I have to manually enter the information. And it has to be done one cell at a time. I can't do the month and year columns together.

Access is built for data entry of one record at a time where that record is treated as separate and standalone and where each component of that record is separate.

Excel is not, which is why I save substantial amounts of time working in Excel first.

(If this doesn't make sense to you now, don't worry. Either you're not so ingrained in working with Excel that it'll be an issue for you or you'll start to understand what I'm talking about as you work in Access. The main caution here is to be careful when working in your data tables that you don't accidentally delete any information or edit information you didn't want to edit. And to think when entering data whether you could do so more effectively in Excel instead of Access.)

Also, the fact that it's so easy to permanently alter a record in Access is why people will advise you to backup your Access database frequently. That way at least if you make some horrible, irreparable mistake you can just go back to the prior version.

I will confess, however, that I don't do this. When I'm about to make a major change to my database I will save a version of the database so that if my change fails I can ditch the new version, but because I keep my raw data elsewhere I know I can always rebuild my entire database in a relatively short period of time. (And maybe even improve on it while I'm at it. Don't be like me, though. It's poor practice to work that way.)

If you're using your Access database for original data entry, though, definitely back up your database every single time you enter new information because you have nowhere else to get that information, so don't risk losing it or overwriting it.

And, seriously, consider what you're doing given your available options in the market today. Is using an Access database in that way really the best idea for your business?

Okay. Enough on that. I hope you get the point.

Now it's time to discuss the basics of working in Access, starting with how to create a new database, save it, delete it, and rename it.

# Absolute Basics

Time to cover how to open, close, save, and rename Access databases.

(If you've read any of the introductory books I've written on Excel, Word, or PowerPoint, you already know most of this, although there are a few key differences when dealing with Access that are worth knowing, so I'd encourage you to at least skim this section if nothing else.)

## Open An Access Database

To start a brand new Access Database, I simply click on Access from my applications menu or the shortcut I have on my computer's taskbar. This opens a home screen where I can then choose Blank Database which is the first option displayed under New.

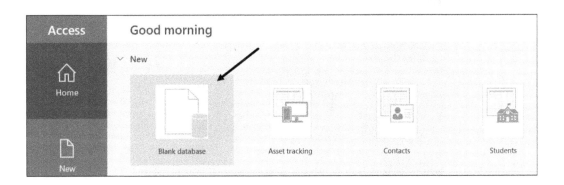

Once you click on that image a dialogue box will appear that allows you to name the database. Type in your name for the database under File Name and then click on the Create button. When you do this, a permanent Access database is created and saved to your computer and then opened for you to work in.

(This is different from Word, Excel, and PowerPoint where the file isn't permanently saved anywhere on your computer until you choose to save it.)

If you'd rather work with a template, Access does provide database templates that you can use instead. As you can see above there are options for asset tracking, contacts, students, and more.

(These would fall under those old-school uses of Access that I don't necessarily recommend because I think there are better products out there to do these sorts of things.)

The templates work the same way as a blank database. Click on the option you want, name the database, and click Create to save the database to your computer and open it. The only difference is that they come with pre-formatted tables to work with.

If you're opening an existing Access file you have a few options. You can go to the folder where the file is saved and double-click on the file name. Or you can open Access and then click on the database name in the Recent section. Or you can open Access and then click on Open from the menu on the left-hand side and navigate from there to where the database is saved.

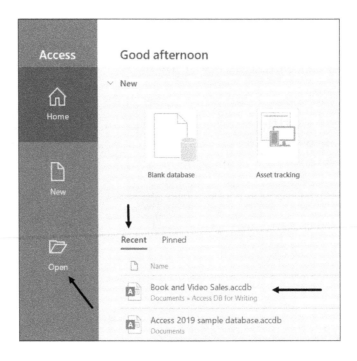

If you click on Open you'll see a list of locations where your files might be stored that includes a Browse option that lets you navigate to anywhere on your computer.

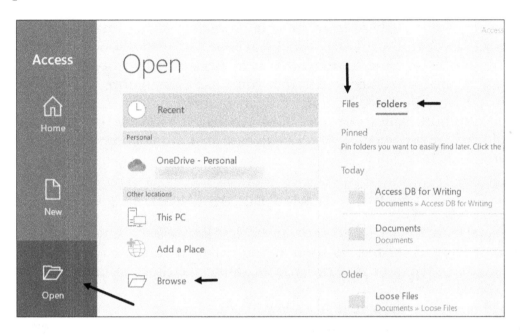

You'll also see a list of Access database files to choose from, listed by when they were last used with pinned databases at the top, and an option to click on folders which will bring up folders where your recently accessed databases were saved.

Clicking on one of those folder names will bring up the Open dialogue box which is the same as what the Browse option does, they just open on a different default location.

If the database you want is listed within the Access start screen, you can left-click to open it. If you open through the dialogue box, either left-click on the database name once to select it and then click on Open or double-click on the database name.

You can also, if you're already in a database, go to the File tab at the top of the screen, click on Open, and then choose the database you need that way.

Unlike Excel, Word, and PowerPoint which let you work with more than one file at a time, Access doesn't let you work in more than one database at a time. If you open a new database it closes the one you were already in.

Also, when you attempt to open a recently-created database Access may display "SECURITY WARNING: Some active content has been disabled. Click for more details" along the top under the menu tabs when the file is reopened.

You don't need to enable that content to see your data, but it means that the database may not be fully functional because certain types of queries or certain macros may not run. If it's a database you created or trust, click on Enable Content.

If you got the database from some questionable source, maybe don't enable content.

(This is a good time to remind you to be sure when opening an Access database created by someone else that you trust them before you click on that option. I have vague recollections of hearing about Access databases that were used to distribute malware or something like that. It happened often enough that I wouldn't willingly open an Access database that didn't come to me through a trusted source.)

## Saving In An Access Database

In general, you don't have to save an Access database the way you do a Word, Excel, or PowerPoint file. As soon as you make an edit to any of your data, it automatically saves so that when you close the file those changes have already been recorded and saved.

I will note here, though, that while you don't have to save the entire database you will need to save any changes you make to the layout of queries, reports, or forms as well as to the formatting of your tables. Access will remind you of this when you close the table, query, report, or form. A dialogue box will appear asking if you want to save your changes. Click yes or no.

To reiterate, this is not asking if you want to save your data. Your data has already been saved. This is asking if you want to keep that column the new width you assigned it or if you want the table to be filtered or sorted the way you just filtered or sorted it.

Even though you don't normally need to save an Access database before closing it, there is still a Save As option which can be used to save a copy of the database under a new name, in a new location, or as a new database file type.

To use that Save As option, click on the File tab and then click on Save As on the left-hand side. Select your database type (I always choose Access Database), and then click on the Save As button. This will bring up the Save As dialogue box where you can choose your location and specify the new database name as needed.

# Delete An Access Database

You can't delete an Access database from within Access. You'll need to navigate to the folder where the database is stored and delete the database there without opening it. (You also can't have it open in Access while trying to delete it.)

Click on the file name to select it and then choose Delete from the menu at the top of the screen, or right-click and choose Delete from the dropdown menu.

# Rename An Access Database

There are two ways to create a version of your Access database with a new name.

First, you can Save As and choose a new name for the database. But that will mean you now have two versions, one with the old name and one with the new name.

Or you can navigate to where you've saved the database. Click on the name once to highlight the name but not open the database. Click on the name a second time to be able to edit the name to whatever you want and do so.

If you change the database name this way there will only be one version of the file, the one with the name you wanted. However, know that you can't then access the database from the Recent listings under Open in the File tab because the name has changed. Even though the database might be listed under its old name, it can no longer be opened. You'll need to open it from the location where it's saved the first time after you change the name.

(This also happens when you move an Access database. Access may list the database still under Recent, but can't open it because it's still looking in the old location for the file. With either a renamed or moved database, you will get a dialogue box that says that Access could not find the file if you click on the database name from within the Access recent file listings.)

# Close An Access Database Or Access

To close an Access database that you have open, just click on the X in the top right corner of Access. You can also go to the File tab and choose Close which will keep Access open but close that specific database. Or you can use Alt + F4 to exit Access and close the database at the same time.

# Basics Of Navigating Access

Now let's cover some basics of navigating within Access.

## See Objects In The All Access Objects Pane

By default the All Access Objects Pane is visible on the left-hand side of your screen and will list all tables, queries, forms, or reports in the current database. If there are more objects than can be shown on the screen, there will be a scroll bar on the right-hand side of the pane that can be used to scroll downward to see the rest of the available objects.

## Collapse An Object Category/Group In The All Access Objects Pane

If you have a large number of objects in the All Access Objects pane, you may want to minimize one category or group of objects (such as tables) to make the rest of the objects more readily visible.

To do so, click on the double upward arrow next to that object category or group. The individual objects in that category will no longer be shown, you'll just see the category or group label.

Another way to do this is to right-click on the category or group name and choose Collapse Group from the dropdown menu to collapse that specific group or Collapse All to collapse all groups at once.

In the image below I've already collapsed the Tables category and have right-clicked on Forms to show the dropdown menu options.

# Expand An Object Category/Group
# In The All Access Objects Pane

To expand a category that you collapsed, click on the double downward facing arrow next to the category label in the All Access Objects pane. You should now see all objects in that category. (You can see this above for the Tables category.)

Or you can right-click on the category label and choose Expand Group from the dropdown menu to expand that specific group or Expand All if you want to expand all of your hidden groups.

# Hide A Category/Group Or Object
# In The All Access Objects Pane

Let me say first, I don't recommend doing this, but someone is bound to want to know how, so let's cover it.

To hide a category of objects, right-click on the category label, and choose Hide from the dropdown menu.

To hide a specific table, query, form, or report, right-click on the object name, and choose Hide in this Group from the dropdown menu.

If the category or object you wanted to hide didn't disappear but was instead just grayed out, see below under Unhide a Category or Object for an explanation.

# Unhide A Category/Group Or Object
# In The All Access Objects Pane

The reason I didn't recommend hiding a category or object is because bringing it back is not as straight-forward as you'd want it to be. In Excel I could hide a worksheet and then right-click on any other worksheet and choose Unhide and go from there. That's not how it works in Access.

You have to go to the All Access Objects header and right-click there to see a dropdown menu that includes Navigation Options. Click on that to bring up the Navigation Options dialogue box.

From there you then need to click the box under Display Options that says "Show Hidden Objects". Click OK and go back to your All Access Objects pane.

Your hidden objects will now show but be grayed out like with the Tables category and Transaction Table Report in the image below:

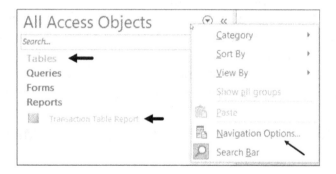

Once you can see a hidden object, you can then right-click on it and choose the Unhide or Unhide in this Group option from the dropdown menu, depending on the type of object.

Note that once you change that navigation option to show hidden objects it will remain changed until you change it again, so if you then hide another object that object will be grayed out but not actually hidden. To truly hide the object you'd need to go back into Navigation Options and uncheck the box to show hidden objects.

M.L. Humphrey

## Rename A Table, Query, Form, Or Report
## In The All Access Objects Pane

To rename any object, right-click on its name in the All Access Objects pane and choose Rename from the dropdown menu. That will allow you to type a new name into the white bar where the current name is.

## Delete A Table, Query, Form, Or Report
## In The All Access Objects Pane

First, let me just caution you that once you're actively using a database I'd advise against deleting an existing data table or query unless you know absolutely that it is not used anywhere and is not needed. Because if you delete that table or query and it's being used in another query, form, or report it will break that other query, form, or report and it's not easy to fix after the fact.

(Fortunately, if you notice right away this is one situation where Ctrl + Z, Undo, actually works to replace the deleted table or query. It will not work to replace a deleted form or report, however.)

To delete an object, right-click on its name in the All Access Objects pane, and choose Delete from the dropdown menu. When Access asks if you're sure you want to do that, say Yes.

Your other option is to click onto the object name in the All Access Objects pane and choose Delete from the Records section of the Home tab.

## Open A Table, Query, Form, Or Report From The All
## Access Objects Pane

Once you've created a table, query, form, or report it will show in the All Access Objects pane on the left-hand side of the screen.

To open a specific table, query, form, or report, double-click on its name or right-click on its name and choose Open from the dropdown menu.

The contents of that table, query, form, or report will now be visible in the main workspace.

# Navigate Between Multiple Open Tables, Queries, Forms Or Reports

You can have more than one object open at a time. When you have more than one table, query, form, or report open at once you can see this because each one will show as a tab in your workspace with the name of the object on the top of the tab. The one you currently have open will be bolded and you will be able to see its contents in the workspace.

To move to another open object, just click on the tab with its name.

Here I have the Transaction Table Report selected so you can see its contents and that its name is bolded in the tab. I also have the Transaction Table, Transaction Table Query, and Transaction Table Form open.

| Transaction Table | Transaction Table Query | Transaction Table Form | **Transaction Table Report** | |
|---|---|---|---|---|

| Transaction Table | | | Saturday, February 20, 2021 |
|---|---|---|---|
| | | | 2:05:40 PM |
| ID | MonthOfSale | YearOfSale | Field3 |
| 2 | February | 2020 | 123 |
| 3 | March | 2020 | |
| 5 | May | 2020 | |
| 6 | June | 2020 | |
| 4 | | | |

Page 1 of 1

# Close An Open Table, Query, Form, Or Report

To close an open table, query, form, or report, right-click on the tab for that object and select Close from the dropdown menu. If you want to close all open objects at once, choose Close All from the dropdown.

You can also click on the X in that same row in the far right-hand corner to close the currently selected object. (If you hold your mouse over the X it should say Close 'Object Name' where Object Name is the name of the object you're about to close.)

## Move Within A Table Or Query In Datasheet View

Datasheet view is the default view for tables and queries. When you're in that view your table or query will look very much like an Excel worksheet with a series of columns and rows.

You can click into any one of the entries in that table or query and then use either the arrow keys or the Tab and Shift + Tab keys to move around to other entries.

Also, the scroll bars can be used to change the information that's visible in the workspace.

You can also use the arrows in the Record section at the bottom of the workspace to move one record forward or backward or to move to the first or last record. I generally use the scroll bars to move through my table and then click on the cell I want, so I don't tend to use this option, but if you're dealing a very large set of data it's probably the easiest way to reach the bottom of your table.

The arrow that is pointing to the right and has a line directly in front of it is the one to use to get to the end of the table. The arrow pointing to the left with a line in front of it is the one to use to get to the top of the table.

You can also type in a specific record number in that section. It will take you to the nth record in the table. Note that this is not tied to the value in the ID column. It will not take you to Record 123, it will take you to the 123rd record.

## Move Within A Form In Form View

The default view for forms is Form View and the default display for forms shows one record at a time.

To move within a specific record, click into an entry on the form and then use Tab and Shift + Tab to move between the fields on that form.

If you are at the last field on the form and you use Tab it will take you to the first field of the next record. If you are at the first field on the form and use Shift + Tab, that will take you to the last field of the prior record. So both of these options in the default layout will take you to a new record.

You can also use the navigation buttons at the bottom of the screen to move between records. The left and right arrows will advance you one record at a time. The arrows with a line will take you to the first or last record's form. And you can enter a value for the record you want and go to that specific record. Keep in mind that the number you enter here is not tied to the ID field. It will take you to the nth record, not Record number N.

## Move Within A Report In Report View

The default view for reports is Report View. You can technically click into a field on your report and then use the Tab and Shift + Tab keys to move from one entry in a report to another, but there's honestly not much point to it because you can't change the values anyway and they're easier to read when you don't have them selected.

The scroll bars on the right-hand side or on the bottom of the workspace will let you see all of the data contained in your report if it fills more than one page.

If your report is in Print Preview, then you will have the page navigation options at the bottom of the screen as discussed above for forms where, in this case, a right or left arrow will move you one printed page at a time, but when you're in the default Report View you just have the scroll bar options.

\* \* \*

Okay. So those were some absolute basics for working with Access. Now let's talk about tables. I'm going to do this a little backwards from how probably anyone else would approach this by starting with how to upload an existing Excel file to create a table rather than how to create a table within Access.

# Tables: Prepare An External Data Source

The way I use Access is based largely upon bringing external data sources into my database, so almost all of my tables are created by uploading an existing data file and then appending additional data to that table over time from external data files.

For me this is primarily .csv files or Excel files. You can upload other types of files, like text files or .XML, but for this book all we're going to cover is .csv and .xls or .xlsx files.

Once your data is uploaded to a table you can then use that table to build queries, forms, or reports. Or you can add summaries, sort, and filter within the table itself. But the first step is to get that data into a table and to do that you need to prepare the data for upload. Let's walk through how to do that.

## Preparing Your Data

First, save a copy of the original file somewhere so that you always have an original version of the file as it existed before you made your changes. That way you can always start over if needed.

Now, open your file because we need to see if the data in the file is ready for upload.

Here, for example, is a mock-up of the first few columns of a file I might receive from one of my vendors:

| | A | B | C | D | E | F |
|---|---|---|---|---|---|---|
| 1 | Date of Sale | Identifier | Title | Publisher | Country of Sale | Currency |
| 2 | 8/1/2017 | 123456789 | A Title | An Author | US | USD |
| 3 | 8/2/2017 | 123456789 | A Title | An Author | US | USD |
| 4 | 8/3/2017 | 123456789 | A Title | An Author | US | USD |
| 5 | 8/6/2017 | 123456789 | A Title | An Author | US | USD |
| 6 | 8/10/2017 | 123456789 | A Title | An Author | US | USD |

The first row contains labels for each column, there are no summary columns on the right-hand side or at the bottom, and no subtotals within the data.

Also, every row of data represents a complete record. Information for a single transaction is stored on a single row. Perfect. This is ready for upload.

Now here's a mockup of what another vendor might send:

| | A | B | C | D | E |
|---|---|---|---|---|---|
| 1 | Title | Author | ASIN | Units Sold | Units Refunded |
| 2 | | | | | |
| 3 | Sales report for the period 01-Aug-2016 to 31-Aug-2016 | | | | |
| 4 | US Store | | | | |
| 5 | A Book | An Author | B123234 | 1 | 0 |
| 6 | A Book | An Author | B123234 | 1 | 0 |
| 7 | Total Royalty for sales on Amazon Kindle US Store (USD) | | | | |
| 8 | | | | | |
| 9 | Title | Author | ASIN | Units Sold | Units Refunded |
| 10 | | | | | |
| 11 | Sales report for the period 01-Aug-2016 to 31-Aug-2016 | | | | |
| 12 | UK Store | | | | |
| 13 | A Book | An Author | B123234 | 1 | 0 |
| 14 | | | | | |
| 15 | | | | | |
| 16 | Title | Author | ASIN | Units Sold | Units Refunded |
| 17 | | | | | |
| 18 | Sales report for the period 01-Aug-2016 to 31-Aug-2016 | | | | |
| 19 | DE Store | | | | |
| 20 | There were no sales during this period | | | | |

This one is a hot mess. The first row is good. We have labels for each column of data.

But then there's a random blank row. And two additional rows of descriptive text related to the next two rows of data. After that Rows 5 and 6 look okay, but they're missing the details that are above in Rows 3 and 4 so my transaction information is split across rows.

And then Row 7 is a summary row that we don't want followed by another blank line, another header row like Row 1, yet another blank line, and then information for the next store. And if you look at Rows 19 and 20 there's information to tell me there's no information for the period for the DE store.

While the first example report could be uploaded as-is, this second report requires a lot of manual adjustments to get it into the proper shape to upload to Access.

This is what happens when someone gives you a report instead of a data extract to work with. For uploading to Access you want raw data without subtotals and totals or pretty little sections and separators.

Ask for just the data, please. One row of column labels followed by one row of information per record with each column in a row containing one specific type of information.

(I discuss how to collect, store, and use the data you need for your business in far more detail in *Data Principles for Beginners* if that's something you need to know. For now, just focus on having one header row and then one row of data per record below that without anything else to muck it up.)

Okay.

So I could upload that first file to Access no problem. Based on the way I use my information I'd probably add two columns, MonthOfSale and YearOfSale, before I did so, but the data as it is is fine.

With the second file I'd have to create a new worksheet. I'd pull over the header information from Row 1 plus add columns for which store the transaction was in as well as the time period. (Or, in my case, the month and year rather than that date range listed in Rows 3, 11, and 18.)

I'd then need to copy the rows that contain the actual transaction information over to my new worksheet. That would be Rows 5, 6, and 13 in this example. And then I'd have to paste in the store and date information.

Which would give me something like this:

| | A | B | C | D | E | F |
|---|---|---|---|---|---|---|
| | | | | | Units | Units |
| 1 | Store | Title | Author | ASIN | Sold | Refunded |
| 2 | US | A Book | An Author | B123234 | 1 | 0 |
| 3 | US | A Book | An Author | B123234 | 1 | 0 |
| 4 | UK | A Book | An Author | B123234 | 1 | 0 |

That I can upload to Access.

If I were creating a file in Excel myself, I'd make sure that each column had its own unique name that was relatively short and fit ideal naming conventions. (For example, Access doesn't like Year or Month for column names.) But when I'm importing from someone else's file, I try to leave the column names alone as much as possible. This is because I plan to then use what I've uploaded into Access as the template each month when I have more data to upload.

The less I move things around and rename them, the easier it is to upload new data.

Also, ideally, the file you use for upload only has one worksheet in it. That saves you the step of having to tell Access which worksheet you want. It's not a deal-breaker, though. If there's more than one worksheet in your file, just be sure you know before you start the upload process what the name of the worksheet you want is so you can select it when the time comes.

If you have data spread across multiple worksheets, you need to upload each worksheet separately. (Although at that point I'm going to say that Excel and Access are not your ideal solutions since you're uploading over a million records.)

# Tables: Upload An Excel File

Okay. So now that you have your data formatted in a way that will work to build a table in Access, it's time to upload that file to Access.

This has changed slightly in Access 2019 so if you ever use an older version of Access expect what you need to do to be located in the same spot in Access, but set up a little different.

In Access 2019, to upload an Excel file, go into your Access database, click on the External Data tab, go to the Import & Link section, and then click on the arrow under New Data Source. This will bring up a dropdown menu. Hold your mouse over From File. This will bring up a secondary dropdown menu. From there, click on Excel.

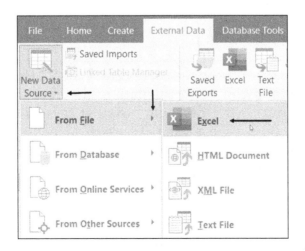

This will bring up the Get External Data – Excel Spreadsheet dialogue box, which looks like this:

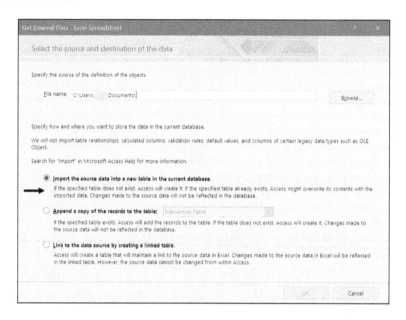

For a new data table, you want to choose the "Import the source data into a new table in the current database" option from the bottom section, which should be the default option.

(If this is your first table in the database there will only be two choices to choose from. If it's not, there will be three choices like in the image above.)

Next, you need to tell Access which file to import. You do this in the top section under where it says "Specify the source of the definition of the objects."

There should be a partial file path already showing. Click on Browse on the right-hand side to bring up the File Open dialogue box. Navigate to where you've saved your source file, click on the file name, and then choose Open.

The File Name should now show the path to the file you selected. Click OK.

At this point you may see a dialogue box that says "The first row contains some data that can't be used for valid Access field names. In these cases, the wizard will automatically assign the field names."

Chances are if you're uploading a data file that wasn't specifically prepared for use in Access that you'll get this message. Since I prefer to keep the names of the columns as close to the original source as possible, I always just let Access make whatever changes it sees fit. But if you really don't like that then make sure your source file has simple names for each column and that those names do not repeat, do not use weird characters, and do not use reserved column names.

For now, if you're like me and you don't care, just click on OK.

On the next screen, Access will bring up the Import Spreadsheet Wizard dialogue box which will show your data split into columns. There is a box for whether or not the first row of your data contains column headings. Often by default it will be checked, but if it isn't and you set up your data like we discussed, then you should check it.

Here is that first vendor report we looked at as an example:

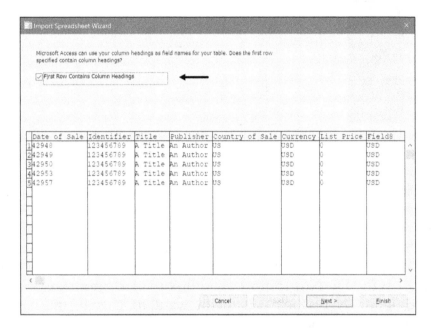

You can see that my first row has been pulled out of the data and used to label each column in the preview. It's the text that's shaded gray.

Below that are the rows of my data. In this example there are five rows of data in the preview and enough columns that they continue on to the right past what's visible.

If you have more data than will fit in the preview section, you can use the scroll bars to move to the right or down to see all of it.

Usually I will just click right through this screen by choosing Next unless something in the preview looks really off. (Sometimes I'll realize on this screen that there was an extra label row or summary row that I forgot to delete, or that I forgot to add the month and year columns to my data, but usually it's fine.)

In the next screen you can choose the format for each column of your data. You can also tell Access not to import a column.

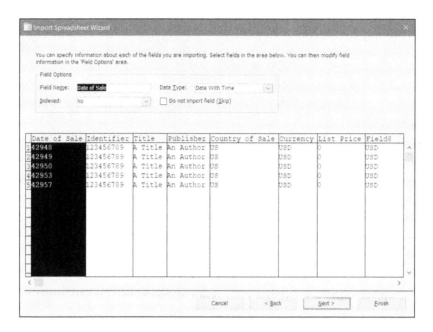

Once again, because I intend to upload more of that type of data into Access later, I try to leave things alone as much as possible because I'm trying to stay as close to the original source of my data as I can.

You can, however, click on each column and see the Data Type that Access has chosen for your data and change that if you need to. For each column you can also click on the Do Not Import Field box to skip importing that field.

There are definitely reasons you might want to change the data type that Access initially assigns to a data field. For example, if you have a zip code field you do not want Access to treat a zip code as a number because it will drop any 0 at the front of the number. A zip code of 06314 will become 6314 and you don't want that.

(We'll discuss the various column formats available in Access later to help you make that choice.)

Once you're done or if you don't want to make any changes, choose Next. That will take you to the screen where you can choose whether or not to have Access add a primary key for you. You have three choices for the primary key: let Access add a primary key, choose one of your columns to serve as the primary key, or don't use one at all.

Unless you have a reason for doing so, my recommendation is to just let Access add the primary key. It does put one more column into your data table (labeled ID) and will make that new column the first column, but it also ensures that every record in your table is unique.

I personally see no harm in having that column in my tables even though I never use it for anything.

Choosing a primary key from the data you're uploading is the best option to use when you're bringing in data that has already been set up with a primary key. For example, a customer contact database where every customer already has a unique Customer ID assigned. In that case, if you already have a field that contains unique values, might as well use it.

Keep in mind, though, that the values in a primary key field must be unique. So, for example, if you had a column in your table with social security number in it and there was a possibility that you could list a customer twice, say they open two accounts with you, then you wouldn't want to use social security number as a primary key even though a social security number is supposed to be unique to an individual.

Most databases assign their own unique identifiers for this reason, because you can't trust that the data you're collecting will in fact be unique.

I should add here that in more traditional database structures tables are often linked based on the primary key in a table such as Customer ID, Product ID, etc.

Of course, that's not how I use Access so primary keys are something I tend to ignore in my own database.

(Don't worry right now if that sounds confusing. We'll come back to this when we build our table relationships.)

One final note. Even though I don't use them, I still wouldn't recommend having no primary key in your table. I can't explain why I feel so strongly about this, but I have some sort of gut-level aversion to creating a table of data that doesn't use a primary key. Unless you have a really good reason, use one.

Okay, then. Once you've made your primary key decision, click Next. Since I usually go with the default, I usually just click Next immediately.

The final screen allows you to name your table. I think it tends to use the worksheet name, so in my example it's showing Sheet2 because I never bothered to change the default name of the worksheet in my file.

If you don't like that name, click in the name field, and change it. Remember that this is what will show in the All Access Objects pane for your table name so make sure it's a name that is descriptive enough for you to know what's in the table.

Once you've done that, click Finish or hit Enter.

(There is a checkbox on that screen that you could've checked to have the wizard analyze your table after importing the data. The only reason to do so is if you're importing a large amount of raw data that you want to split into multiple tables to avoid the duplication of data and aren't sure how to split it or want

Access to do that for you. Since I don't use Access that way, I don't use this option. Even if I did, I'm a control freak and probably wouldn't trust Access to know the difference between values that are repetitive and can be split out vs. values that look repetitive but need to remain part of each transaction record, such as price.)

Once you click Finish you'll then see one more screen where you can save your import steps. I never do, so I just click on Close or the X in the corner to close the dialogue box.

At this point Access will upload your data and create a table from it. You can see the table in the All Access Objects pane on the left-hand side of the screen under the Tables category. To see the data that was imported, double-click on the table name and you'll see your data in Datasheet View in the main workspace.

Sometimes there are errors in uploading data to a table. Access will tell you that there are errors and give you the choice of continuing. If you do so, there may also be a table called [TableName]$_ImportErrors that is created where TableName is whatever you chose to name your table.

You can open that table to see what errors occurred in the upload. For me, this happens with N/A values in tables. Access can't import N/A values so leaves those fields blank. I know this, so I let it import anyway and just check the import errors table to make sure that the rows and fields listed as having errors correspond to the N/A values in my table. (I could just as easily do a find and replace in Excel before I upload to avoid the error message and table creation.)

With a new data table it's always good to spot check any import errors to make sure crucial information wasn't lost and to understand what data Access couldn't handle in its import.

Finally, I always open my newly-created table to do a spot check and see if it all looks alright. I shouldn't see blank records, for example. And I expect all of the values in each column to look the same and for the values in the fields to make sense given the column names.

That was how to upload an Excel file. Now let's cover how to upload a .csv file type instead.

# Tables: Upload A .CSV File

I honestly don't upload .csv files all that often because when I open them in Excel to make sure that there isn't excess information that needs to be fixed I usually end up saving the resulting file as an Excel file.

But you can upload a .csv file, so let's walk through how to do that.

In your Access database go to the External Data tab and click on the arrow under New Data Source in the Import & Link section. Hold your mouse over From File and choose Text File from the secondary dropdown menu.

The first screen is going to look exactly like the one we saw above with Excel file uploads except it's called the Get External Data – Text File dialogue box. Make sure the option to import your source data into a new table is selected and then use the Browse option to select the file you want to import.

Note that with both the Excel and the Text option when you navigate to a file location you will only see files of that type. For example, in this case when I navigated to where I had both an Excel version and a .csv version of my file I could only see the .csv version.

After you've selected your file, click on OK to move to the next screen.

You will now see the Import Text Wizard which is where you tell Access how your data in your .csv file is separated, Delimited or Fixed Width.

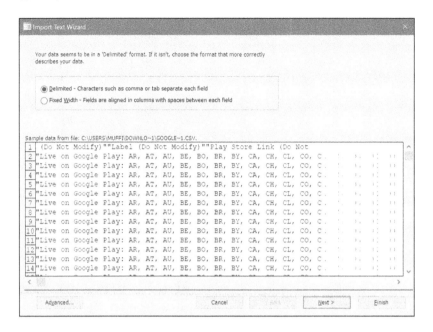

Usually the data will be delimited, meaning it's separated with a tab or a comma or some other identifiable character. Fixed Width data is data that always takes up the same number of characters for each field.

From what you can see of the above .csv file if I didn't have a header row I could probably use either option because all of the visible fields have the same width for each column, but I happen to know that not all of the fields will be the same width. Also, the header row is clearly not the same number of characters as the entries below.

Even though you can see your data as it looks in the .csv file in the preview section you won't actually be able to tell whether you chose the right option until you click on Next at the bottom of the page and specify your delimiter or field width. Until you do that the data is shown in its raw format.

(This is different from Excel which when you use Get & Transform Data, From Text/CSV will show you a preview with the data already parsed into separate columns.)

When you choose the Delimited option, the next screen will have you identify what character is being used as your delimiter. Access will try to make that choice for you, but it may not get it right. For example, with this data file the right choice was tab, but Access tried to use comma. To change the selected delimiter just click on the white bubble for the one you want.

Once the correct delimiter has been chosen your data will appear in the preview section in columns that are separated with a line.

The column labels and column contents should make sense.

Here you can see the end of one column that lists every country where each book is for sale, a column that shows the type of upload settings used for that book, and the beginning of a column that contains a link to each book in the store.

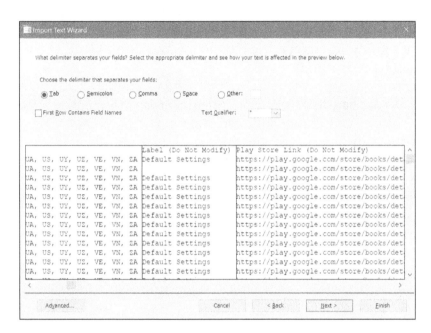

There's still one issue that needs to be fixed here. As you can see, the first line of data, which contains the field names, is the same color as the other rows of data. Access did not automatically identify that there was a header row. To make Access do so, check the "First Row Contains Field Names" box just under the delimiter section.

(When I did that, Access gave me the same warning message it did with the Excel file that some of my column names weren't suitable as field names and that it would assign them for me. I just said OK.)

If your data was fixed width instead, then this screen would require you to insert lines to show where the breaks in your data should be. Access will attempt to do so itself, but you will likely need to move those lines around.

To move an existing line, click on it and drag. To delete a line, double-click on it. To add a line, click in the sample area at the spot where you want to insert the line. Each line represents the beginning of a new column.

With either option, make sure your data looks "right" in the preview before you click on Next to move to the next screen.

The next screen is identical to the one with the Excel upload where you can choose to format your data or not import a field. Access will sometimes assign a different format to values that are uploaded direct from a .csv file compared to when the same file is opened in Excel and saved as a .xls or .xlsx file first. For example, a number field may be assigned the Double field type when uploaded via Excel but the Long Integer field when uploaded direct from the .csv file.

As mentioned above, I generally will leave the assigned field type alone unless I know that it's going to change the data in a way I don't want, such as a zip code formatted as a type of number field.

When you're done with you formatting choices click Next. This will take you to a primary key screen that is also identical to the one you see when uploading an Excel file. Make your choice and click Next.

Change your table name if you need to and then click Finish. Make your decision about saving your import steps (I never do) and click Close. The new table will be added to your database.

One thing to note here.

If you upload a new table and there is already a table by that name in your database, you will get an error message asking if you want to overwrite the existing table.

If you say Yes that will overwrite your existing table. All of the data that already existed in that table will be lost. You cannot get it back. If you get that error message, be very very certain that you want to overwrite whatever data table you already have before clicking Yes.

Chances are you do not want to do that and would be better off choosing No and then giving the table a different name. This is what I always do, because I know that I can always delete the old table manually later if it turns out I no longer need it.

(We'll talk about this more later, but if for some reason you really did want to replace all of the contents of an existing table, I would probably recommend selecting all the existing records, deleting them, and then uploading the new data into that table using the append option.)

Okay.

Just like with uploading an Excel file you will now have a table that contains your data in the Tables section of the All Access Objects pane. Regardless of the source file type (Excel or .csv or other), once the information is added into Access it's just a data table. There's no difference in overall structure based on the source file and at a quick glance no way to see that one table was created with an .xlsx file and another was created with a .csv file.

# Tables: Export An Existing Table To Excel

In the next chapter we'll discuss how to upload additional data to an existing table. My first step when I'm going to do this is to export a current copy of the table I'm adding data to as an Excel file. Let's walk through how to do that now.

To export a table from Access to Excel, click on the table name, go to the External Data tab, and click on Excel in the Export section.

I always choose "Export Data With Formatting and Layout" and also choose to open the destination file after the export operation is complete.

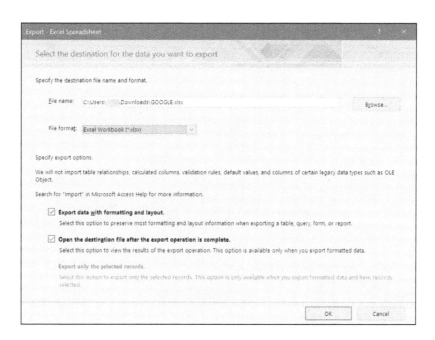

If you don't tell it to open the destination file afterward, you'll have to find the file wherever it exported to, which is shown in the File Name box at the top. You can change that location with the Browse option. It appears to default to wherever you last imported from, so in this case it's showing my Downloads folder.

You can also choose from the file format dropdown to change the file type from the default .xlsx file format to .xls or even .xlsb. (I have never personally needed .xlsb but would need .xls if someone I was working with had a pre-2007 version of Excel.)

Click on OK once you've made your selections. If you chose to open the file, Excel will open and display the data from your table in an Excel worksheet.

There will also be a dialogue box in Access asking if you want to save your export steps. I never do, so I just click on Close. (Alt + Tab is an easy way to move back and forth between your Excel file and your Access database.)

# Tables: Upload Data To An Existing Table

Because I usually work with outside data sources, the way I normally add data to an existing table is by uploading a new Excel file to my database and appending that data to my table rather than by manually entering data directly in Access.

I often have hundreds or thousands of rows of data to bring in at once and manual entry is just not an option I want to consider.

Since I may have changed the data type for one of my fields and because sometimes my vendors change the layout of their reports with no notice, I always start by exporting the table I want to work with to an Excel file.

(I can easily export my data tables because they are relatively small. If you have very large sets of data, you could use a query that uses all fields from a data table but just a small subset of the records and export that. The goal is to have an Excel file with the exact same columns as your data table and at least one row of formatted data.)

I then open that file and delete all of the data except the top two rows. The top row is the header row, the next row is my first row of data. If the table used an ID column I will also delete that.

(A quick way to select a range of records in Excel is to click in the top left cell of the range that you want (in my case Cell A3), hold down Shift + Ctrl, then use the down arrow and the right arrow to select the entire range. Once you've done that you can use the Delete key to delete the data or right-click and choose Delete from the dropdown menu.

That should leave you with something like this:

| | A | B | C | D | E | F |
|---|---|---|---|---|---|---|
| 1 | Identifier | tus (Do Not Mod | el (Do Not Mod | re Link (Do Not | Enable for Sale? | Title |
| 2 | GGKEY:0F3: | Live on Google P | Default Settings | https://play.goo | Yes | A New |
| 3 | | | | | | |

If you built your initial table using your external data source as your template, you should now be able to go to that external data source, select the data you need, paste it into this document, and have it match column for column.

(That's why I try not to adjust data even if there are columns I know I don't need. Because if I delete columns in my Access tables then I have to remember to delete those columns again every single time I upload new data from that source.)

When I paste from my vendor reports, I copy and paste the header row as well as the data I want so that I can compare my column headers and make sure that everything lines up.

I paste the information from my source file into the downloaded Excel file starting in Row 4. I then compare my column headers between the data table from Access and the data that I've just pasted into the document to make sure they match.

If there is a mismatch you can go back to Access and add, delete, or move a column around to get the table fields to match the data you're going to import. Generally, I don't like to delete data that's already in my database, but if it's a field you know you aren't using, you can do that.

I try to adjust the table in Access because I know that chances are the data I'm bringing in is going to be formatted however it's formatted going forward. Changing my imported data instead would mean that I have to make that change every time I import new data.

There are times when I do have to adjust the import file. For example, one of my vendors reports two types of sales in the same column. They report paid sales as well as a number for pages read which are two entirely different numbers. The way I've built my database relies on splitting those values into separate columns. So every month with that vendor I have to make that adjustment.

You'll need to decide which file to adjust given your own circumstances. But I will say that no matter how many times I've already uploaded data from an existing source, I perform this check.

And I'm glad I do. Because every one of my vendors has made an unannounced change to their data file and this is where I caught the difference which is a better place to catch it than in your summary reports.

Okay. So, once I've confirmed that my columns match, the next thing I do is apply the Format Painter from Row 1 (which is the formatting and data type that came from my Access data table) down to the new rows of data that I've just pasted into the table. For me this starts at Row 5, right below the pasted-in column names.

(To use the Format Painter, select Row 1, click on the Format Painter brush in the Clipboard section of the Home tab, and then select all of your rows of data that you want to sweep that formatting to.)

What this should do is make sure that the data type for the data you're bringing in to Access matches the data type of what you already have there.

Next I delete Rows 2 through 4 which are the old data I kept in Row 2 for its formatting, a blank row, and the header row from the data I'm importing.

That leaves me with a header row in Row 1 that came from Access and so will match my existing field names followed by all of my new data that I need to import.

I save the Excel file, go back to Access, go to the External Data tab, click on the arrow under New Data Source in the Import & Link section, and from the File option in the dropdown menu choose Excel.

This brings up the Get External Data – Excel Spreadsheet dialogue box that you've seen before.

In the File Name section use the Browse button to find the file you want to upload. It should default to looking where you last exported to which means it's usually going to already be pointing to the folder that has your file.

What is different this time is that I choose the second option in the bottom section, "Append a copy of the records to the table."

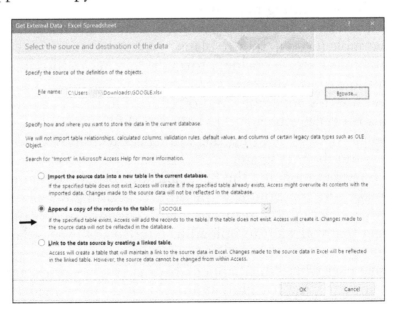

When I click on that option I'm given access to a dropdown menu where I can choose which existing table I want to append the data to.

I choose the table I originally exported from and click OK. (Because of the way I do this the file name in the Browse section usually matches the dropdown choice.)

I quickly look on the next screen to make sure there isn't anything I've missed or messed up. (I add columns for month and year to all of my data and if I forget to add those values into my table this is where I'll notice it because I'll have two glaringly blank columns.)

If everything looks good, then I click Next and then Finish to complete the upload steps. (Or really you can probably just click Finish in the second screen.)

Ninety-five times out of a hundred that's all it will take to upload data to an existing table. The data is added onto the end of the entries that were already there so will always be at the bottom.

I open the table to confirm that they're there and that they look okay.

There can be times using this method when Access imports blank rows along with the data I wanted. If that happens I select those rows and delete them.

* * *

Every once in a while this process does not work.

Usually when it doesn't work I get a "Subscript Out of Range" error message. It's not a helpful error message because it doesn't tell you what you need to fix and doing an internet search for explanations doesn't provide much clarity.

Sometimes it's a formatting mismatch.

Sometimes it seems to be Access seeing columns of data outside of what it expects for that table (even if they're blank).

I think sometimes it can be using a formula and Access not knowing how to handle that formula.

But whatever it is, it's annoying. And often hard to fix.

If you used a formula, you can go to your Excel file, copy all of your data, and then paste special–values back into the worksheet to remove the formulas and keep the values, and then try again.

You can also try downloading the file again and format sweeping to your new data again to make sure that you have the same formatting for all of your entries.

Or you can try deleting a handful of blank columns and blank rows at the edge of the data that you want to upload to remove any excess data that Access may think is there.

I have one data set where this happens because the vendor started putting X at the end of some of the formerly-numeric values. It's a field I don't use for anything so I can just delete those entries with the X in them and that file will then upload just fine. (I could probably just change the format of the field, too, but I'm oddly lazy at times.)

Sometimes none of the above works.

When that's the case, I upload the data into a new table and then copy and paste all rows from that table into my existing table using Paste-Append.

To do this, follow the steps to import the source data into a new table. Be sure to name the worksheet that you're uploading something different from your existing table otherwise you may overwrite the existing table.

Leave all column formatting and names alone (because you should've already applied that formatting when you were trying to append this data to the existing table and the column names should already be what's in the table in Access). So just Next, Next, Next, Finish.

Open your new data table, use Ctrl + A to select all the records and Ctrl + C to copy them.

Next, open the table where you actually wanted the records to go, and click into the first cell in the bottom row of that table.

From the Clipboard section of the Home tab, click on the arrow under Paste, and choose Paste Append. Access will tell you you're about to paste X number of records. Click on Yes.

As long as your columns match up between the two tables, you should have no issue with pasting the data over this way.

If the columns don't match you will get a lot of error messages about how you're trying to paste numeric data as text or vice versa. Cancel out as soon as you can, because clearly there is a mismatch between the data you're trying to bring in and the data you already have. To figure out why that is, you'll need to look at both tables in Design View and determine where they don't match. (We'll cover views in a minute, don't worry.) And you'll need to change the data type for one or the other and then try to paste again.

If the copy and paste worked, you can delete the second table that was created when you uploaded the new data. Everything should now be in the original table.

It probably sounds messy. And it is. But it works. And many times I've found it easier to add my data to Access this way than to try and figure out where that error message was coming from.

# Tables: Create One From Scratch

The more traditional way to create a table in a self-contained database is to create it within Access. I'd say I only do this about 5% of the time, but I do need to do it on occasion. Let's quickly walk through how to do so.

First, go to the Create tab and choose Table from the Tables section.

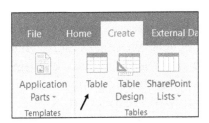

This will create for you a basic table with one column/field, ID, and the ability to add additional columns/fields. The second column/field shown says "Click to Add". Left-click on the arrow at the end of the column name to choose the type of field you want it to be. If you're unsure, Short Text is usually a safe choice. (We'll go through field data types in the next chapter.)

Access will add your new column and highlight the name, which for the first field you add will be Field1 so that you can change it. Just type your new column name and hit Enter.

Repeat this process until you have all of your desired columns/fields added to the table.

(One word of warning when naming fields/columns. There are certain words that Access considers reserved words which "have a specific meaning to Microsoft Access or to the Microsoft Access database engine". If you use one of them Access will caution you that you may receive an error when referring to the field. I've seen this error with respect to Name, Month, and Year but have managed to use all three without a problem. Best practice is to not use them, though. So, for example, use MonthOfSale instead of Month. There's a fairly extensive list of some of the reserved words that you can access by clicking on Help when this message appears, but there are more reserved words than are listed.)

\* \* \*

To add data into a table, click into or navigate to the cell where you want to type your value and type it in and then use Enter or the tab or arrow keys to move to the next cell.

If you try to enter a value that isn't the same as the format you chose for that column you will get an error message and not be able to enter your value.

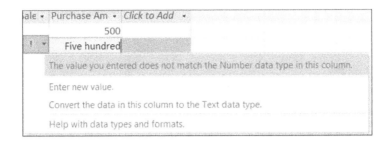

For example, in this case I made the third column Purchase Amount using a number data type and then tried to enter my value as text. Access wasn't willing to accept that and told me so. (It will however accept numbers added into a text field since text fields are actually alphanumeric, but if you do that those numbers are treated as text and can't be used in calculations.)

To fix that issue, delete your entry or replace it with an entry that does match the data type for the field.

I wouldn't generally recommend converting your data type unless your database is brand new.

* * *

That's it. Pretty easy to create a basic table and add data to it.

# Field Data Types

Now we need to discuss field data types.

Whether or not you can do something in Access will be driven by the data type assigned to that field. If a field is designated as text, you won't be able to have Access provide you a sum of the values in that field, for example. Other data types have limitations on how much text you can enter or on what text you can enter or will convert a decimal number you enter to a whole number, so getting your data types "right" can be important.

Many of the below data types can be further refined in the Design View, which we'll discuss in the next chapter. For now, just note when I refer to the Design View and we'll come back to it in a moment.

Okay. The main data types are:

## Short Text

(In versions prior to Access 2013 this was referred to as just Text.)

This data type can be used for short, alphanumeric values. This means it can have both numbers and text. The default field size is 255 characters which is about the length of a single paragraph.

It's also a good choice for any numeric value that won't be used in calculations, like a phone number. And should be used for numbers where there is a zero in the front, such as zip codes.

## Long Text

(In versions prior to Access 2013 this was referred to as Memo.)

Long Text is used for lengthier combinations of text and numbers. It can take up to 64,000 characters which is about 175 average-sized paragraphs of text.

When using Access as a desktop database (which is what we're covering in this book), Long Text fields can be set to display formatting like bold and underline if you change the Text Format option in the Design View to Rich Text.

# AutoNumber

AutoNumber is used for primary keys and the ID field. It assigns a unique numeric value to the next record (row) in the table. Normally this value will start at 1 and increase by 1 each time. It cannot be updated once assigned and the number also cannot be reused. If you cut a record and paste it back into your table, it will be assigned the next number in sequence, it will not keep its original value.

You can change the settings so that Access instead assigns a random unique value to each new record instead of increasing the number by 1 each time. You do this in Design View under New Values where you change the setting from Increment to Random. When I did this, the next value it assigned was 1063737268 instead of 4.

Honestly, I don't think I'd use that setting, but it is there and if you're thrown by the occasional missed record number because of a deleted record this is certainly one way to eliminate that. It is not retroactive, however, so if you already have records listed in your table and want them to also have lengthy, random ID values, you'll need to cut and paste-append the records back into your table.

# Number

Number is the field type to use for normal numeric values where a mathematical calculation may be performed.

Within the Design View you can choose different field sizes for the Number field. The most common are Double and Long Integer.

You can also have Byte, Integer, Single, and Decimal field sizes for Number.

Depending on the size type you choose, there will be limitations. Some, for example, do not allow decimals. And some work in a very narrow range of values.

The following is from the Access Help descriptions for field size.

Byte stores integers from 0 to 255. No fractions/decimals are allowed.

Integer stores integers from -32,768 to 32,767. No fractions/decimals are allowed.

Long Integer stores integers from -2,147,483,648 to 2,147,483,647. No fractions/decimals are allowed.

Decimal stores numbers from -9.999…x 1027 to +9.999.. x 1027. (So basically very large numbers in both a negative and a positive direction.) It can be precise up to 28 decimals.

Single stores numeric values with a floating decimal point from -3.4 x 1038 up to 3.4 x 1038. It can be precise up to seven significant digits.

Double stores numeric values with a floating decimal point from -1.797 x 10308 up to 1.797 x 10308. It can be precise up to fifteen significant digits.

Using Number types that take up less storage size requires less memory and can improve processing times. If that's an issue for you, Decimal and Double take up the most storage space. Byte and Integer take up the least.

(Now you can maybe understand why I prefer to import my data into Access and let it choose the best number data type for the data rather than try to make that decision myself up front.)

## Large Number

The Large Number data type is new in Access 2019 and, according to Access, can be used to efficiently calculate large numbers. It is not compatible with older Access databases, however.

According to Access, the Number data type has a range from $-2^{31}$ to $2^{31}-1$ when performing calculations whereas the Large Number data type has a range from $-2^{63}$ to $2^{63}-1$.

I would suspect that most users will not need the Large Number data type and should stick with Number because of backwards compatibility with prior versions of Access.

## Currency

The Currency field type is for monetary values and will include a comma for the thousands separator as well as following regional Windows settings for negative amounts, decimal and currency symbols, and decimal places.

(So for me 1234.56 becomes $1,234.56, for example.)

The Currency field is accurate to 15 digits to the left of the decimal point and to 4 digits to the right.

In the Format field under Design View you can choose various ways for your Currency field to display. Access recommends using the default Currency format in most instances, but if you need, for example, the Euro sign and are in the U.S.

or if you don't want a dollar sign used, you can change that selection in the dropdown menu. There are examples of each formatting choice so you can see what you're choosing.

(This is probably a good time to point out to you the dangers of storing data in more than one currency in your Access database. I don't think Access is really set up to handle multiple currencies well. Also, if you poke around you'll see that there have been issues for users who try to use the same database but in different geographies. I personally only work in USD in my database which matches to my regional settings. To avoid working in multiple currencies in Access even though my sales reports come in multiple currencies, I convert all of my foreign currency values to USD before I upload any data to my Access database.)

## Date/Time

The Date/Time field provides date and time values for the years 100 through 9999. There is now a Date/Time Extended field type that provides date and time values for the years 1 through 9999, but it is not compatible with earlier versions of Access.

(Be careful here, because Excel has different date parameters than Access and can't work with the same range of dates as Access can. If for some reason you are working with dates in the 1800s or 1700s or earlier and export your file from Access to Excel, Excel will not handle those dates properly. The date will export as a negative number which Excel cannot convert into a date. It will just show up in the Excel file as a bunch of ############ signs.)

A Date/Time field can be further formatted in Design View as General Date, Long Date, Medium Date, Short Date, Long Time, Medium Time, and Short Time. Most users will likely prefer Medium Date or Short Date. You can see a sample for each option in the dropdown menu.

## Yes/No

The Yes/No data type only allows for one of two values and by default shows as a checkbox where a check is Yes and no check is No.

You can change that to True/False or On/Off.

To display text instead of a check box, go to Design View, click on the Lookup tab, and then choose Combo Box or Text Box under the Display Control dropdown.

A value of 1 can be entered to indicate Yes/True/On. A value of 0 can be entered to indicate No/False/Off.

* * *

There are other data types for Lookup & Relationship, Rich Text, Attachment, Hyperlink, and Calculated Field but those are more advanced data types that we're not going to cover here.

# Table Views

The default for viewing a table of data is the Datasheet View. That's the one with your actual data values displayed in rows and columns, like so:

| Custom Table | | | | | | |
|---|---|---|---|---|---|---|
| ID ▾ | FirstName ▾ | MonthOfSale ▾ | Purchase Am ▾ | DateOfPurch ▾ | Current Cust ▾ | Click to Add ▾ |
| 521865984 | 123 | | | 1/1/1901 | True | |
| 1063737268 | asdasda | | $0.00 | 1/1/1701 | False | |
| 1727406757 | asdas | | $0.00 | | False | |
| 1822708994 | Mary | March | $500.00 | | False | |
| 1856010266 | Charles | April | $1.00 | | True | |
| 1942142299 | Bob | July | $100.00 | | False | |
| * (New) | | | $0.00 | | False | |

But there is another view available with respect to tables, the Design View. You access this view by going to the Views section of the Home tab, clicking on the dropdown arrow under View, and choosing Design View.

This is what your table of data turns into when you do so:

| Custom Table | | | ✕ |
|---|---|---|---|
| **Field Name** | **Data Type** | **Description (Optional)** | |
| ID | AutoNumber | | |
| FirstName | Short Text | | |
| MonthOfSale | Short Text | | |
| Purchase Amount | Currency | | |
| DateOfPurchase | Date/Time | | |
| Current Customer | Yes/No | | |

This top section is still a table of information, but now what you see listed is the Field/Column information instead of your data. The first column is the Field Name, the second column is the Data Type for that field, and the third column allows you to type in a description of what information is contained in that field.

(If multiple users are going to use your database and it's not clear what a field does or contains, providing a description can be very helpful.)

Let's walk through a few rows here. The first row is the field ID, which has a little key sign on the left-hand side because it's the primary key field for the table. The data type shown is AutoNumber.

The last row shown there is described as Current Customer and is a Yes/No field. (If I were designing this database for other users I'd add a description that said, "Indicates whether the customer listed is a current customer or not.")

Now let's look at the area below the table in Design View. This is the Field Properties section which is where you can make additional choices with respect to your Data Type.

(You can also add things like Validation Rules, Default Values, etc. which we aren't going to cover here but are covered in *Access 2019 Intermediate*.)

| Field Properties | | |
|---|---|---|
| **General** Lookup | | |
| Field Size | 255 | |
| Format | | |
| Input Mask | | |
| Caption | | |
| Default Value | | |
| Validation Rule | | |
| Validation Text | | The maximum number of characters you can enter in the field. The largest maximum you can set is 255. Press F1 for help on field size. |
| Required | No | |
| Allow Zero Length | Yes | |
| Indexed | No | |
| Unicode Compression | Yes | |
| IME Mode | No Control | |
| IME Sentence Mode | None | |
| Text Align | General | |

So here is the Field Properties section for the FirstName field which has a data type of Short Text. Each data type will have different options listed in this section. As you can see, Short Text has a number of them.

Above I've clicked into the box for Field Size. The text off to the right-hand side describes what this option does. In this case, Access tells me that Field Size determines "the maximum number of characters you can enter in the field." The definition further informs me that 255 is the largest size I can set.

Here's an example of what the Field Properties section looks like for Currency.

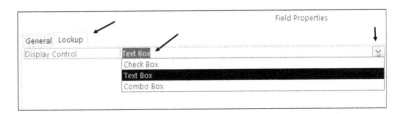

You can see it doesn't have a Field Size option but instead starts with Format which is a dropdown menu. I've clicked on that dropdown arrow to show the various available currency formats.

As a beginner you'll probably stick to field size or format, but for the Yes/No data type if you want to change the checkbox to text you'd click on the tab for Lookup and then click into the Display Control option box to bring up a dropdown menu that lets you change that option from Check Box to Text Box, like so:

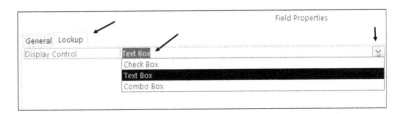

As mentioned above, the Field Properties section is also where you can specify a display format for your data, a caption to use in place of the field name, a default value for the field, validation rules to apply when entering data in that field, whether the field must be completed or not for each record, whether to index values in the field, and how to align the text in the field for display purposes.

But we're not going to get into that here, because that's beyond the basic analysis I wanted to cover in this book. It's more for when you have multiple users inputting data into your table directly which is why it's covered in *Access 2019 Intermediate*. For now just know where those options are located in case you do for some reason need them.

I will add that the most frequent change I have to make in Design View for a table is to change the data type of a field I've imported where the value is a numeric value that I need to make calculations with but where Access assigned a data type of Short Text.

One other note. If size or processing speeds are issues for you (which they shouldn't be at a beginning level), changing your field settings to a smaller field size can help. BUT, be very careful doing so for an existing database. Access will have to go through and make that change to all of your existing fields, which could hang up or crash your database. (It might be better to export the data into Excel and bring it back into a new table that has the settings you want to use.)

Also, if you change a data type after you have data in your table you may lose data. For example, if you have a value of 1.23456 and apply one of the Number formats that don't allow decimals, you'll be left with a value of 1 which may not be what you want.

Just to give you an example of what can happen with one of these changes, I took a Short Text field and put the values "United States" and "US" into fields in a column and then went to the Design View and changed the field size to 2.

Access did give me an error message that I'd changed the size of one or more fields to a shorter size and data might be lost, but all it mentioned was that a validation rule might be violated as a result.

I went ahead and saved the change, and when I went back to my data table my entry that previously read "United States" was now "Un".

There was no way to undo that change at that point. If I'd done that in a table with thousands of records, imagine how much data I would've lost and been unable to recreate. That "Un" could've been "United Kingdom" just as easily as "United States" so there'd be no way to back into the values I lost.

(This is another reminder of why I like to keep my raw data elsewhere rather than use Access for primary data entry.)

The other issue with adjusting field size or type is that once you do so, Access will not allow you to input a value that is outside of that range or of a different type.

So when my Small Text field allowed 255 characters I could easily type in United States, but the minute I changed it to 2 characters and saved it, I was stuck with just two characters in that field.

Only make those kinds of changes if you are sure you know what you're doing. If you aren't, save a backup of your database before you begin, so you don't lose crucial information if you make a mistake. Access is much less forgiving than Excel in this respect.

Okay, so that's how the Design View works with respect to tables. We'll circle back to Design View later for Queries, but first I want to cover how to amend records in tables.

# Amend Records and Fields In Tables

Alright. Now that we have a table that we've uploaded into Access or created manually and that table has some data in it, it's time to walk through how to amend the data in your table.

I should note here that most of what we're going to discuss with respect to tables also can apply to certain types of queries, but I would not recommend adding, deleting, copying, cutting, or pasting records in queries since doing so will impact your underlying data table. If you delete a record in a basic detail query, it's deleted from the data table as well.

To be properly in control of what you're doing to your data, I'd make it a habit to always amend data through a table or a form and never through a query even when it's possible to do so.

Okay. So the basics of handling data in an existing table.

## Add A New Record To A Table

To add a new record to a table, go to the last row of your table and start typing in your data. There will be a star on the far left side of that row to indicate it's the row where you can add a new record. If the table is using an AutoNumber ID field for its primary key, you will start entering your data in the next column/ field over.

If the table is particularly large, you can right-click on the gray box on the left-hand side of any existing row/record and choose New Record from the dropdown menu and that will take you to the bottom of the table where you can then add a new record. Another option is to click anywhere in the table and then choose New from the Records section of the Home tab.

Or you can use the Record navigation options at the bottom of the table and click on the right-pointing arrow with a line in front of it to go to the last record and then arrow down to the next row from there.

As you enter your text and hit Enter the cursor will move to the next column over. You can also use the Tab or the right arrow keys to move between fields.

If you enter a value in a field that isn't allowed for that field you will get an error message that the value you entered does not match the data type of the column. Choose Enter New Value and type in a value that does work for that field or delete your entry.

If you're not sure what will work for the field, delete your current entry, change your view to Design View and see what data type has been assigned to it.

The error dropdown also may have an option to convert the data in that column to a data type that will work for your entry, but as always be very careful converting a field that's already in use since you may lose crucial data by doing so.

## Add a New Field to a Table

To add a new field to your table, right-click on an existing column/field and choose Insert Field. This will insert a new field to the left-hand side of the column you right-clicked on when you chose Insert Field.

The field will need to be renamed (see below) and you may need to change the Data Type in the Design View screen.

You can also go to the end of the table and left-click on the "Click to Add" option in the last column and choose the type of new field you want to add from the dropdown menu. This will add the field as the last column in the table.

A third option for inserting a new field is to click onto a column/field in your table and go to the Add & Delete section of the Fields tab under Table Tools. Select the Data Type you want, and it will insert a new column/field into the table with that assigned Data Type.

The new column will be inserted to the right of the column you were clicked onto in the table.

## Move a Field

If a field/column is in your table but you want to move it to another location in that table, left-click on the field name to select it and then left-click again at the bottom edge of the field name so that you see a dark-colored solid line on the left-hand side.

Hold down that left-click and drag the column to where you want it.

That dark-colored line will move so that it's along the edge of the border between two columns. That's where the column you're moving will go when you release your left-click.

Be sure you drag the column far enough to actually move it, because the first black line you see will keep it right where it is.

If that method doesn't work, hold your mouse over the bottom edge of the name of the column you want to move until your cursor becomes a four-sided arrow. (Sometimes it's easier to make the four-sided arrow appear if you click on the column name first.)

Once you see the four-sided arrow, click and drag the column to its new location as described above.

(And remember that if you're primarily working with data you upload from other sources into Access that moving around your columns will impact the ease of uploading more data into that table since you'll have changed the order of your columns. This can be useful though when, for example, a vendor eliminates a column from their reports but you still want to keep the data you already had in that column.)

Another option is to move the column in Design View.

To do so, go to Design View and then left-click on the gray box to the left of the field name and drag the field up or down to its new location. A black line will show where the column is going to be when you let go of the left-click. When you save and return to Datasheet View the column should be in its new location.

(It's easier to move a column this way for me but it's not as easy to visualize how it will look when I'm done and since it requires moving back and forth between Design View and Datasheet View I rarely use this method.)

## Rename a Field

To change a field name, right-click on the top of the column and choose Rename Field from the dropdown menu. This will highlight the existing field name. Type in the new name you want to use and hit Enter. (You cannot use Undo to reverse this change once you've made it.)

You can also go to Design View, click into the cell for that column under Field Name, and change it there. As with any change you make in Design View you'll need to agree to save the change before you can return to the Datasheet View.

# Delete a Record From a Table

To delete a record from a table, right-click on the gray box on the far left-hand side of the row where that record is stored and choose Delete Record from the dropdown menu.

You can also select the record and then use the Delete option in the Records section of the Home tab.

Access will present you with a dialogue box that says "You are about to delete 1 record(s). If you click Yes, you won't be able to undo this Delete operation. Are you sure you want to delete these records?" Click on Yes if you are. Click on No if you don't want to delete the record after all.

# Select a Record or Records In a Table

To select a single record (row) in a table, click on the gray box to the left of the first field for that row. The row that is selected will be highlighted in blue.

To select multiple records that are next to one another, click on the gray box to the left of the first column/field for either the topmost row or the bottommost row and then hold down the left-click as you drag downward or upward until all of the rows you want are selected.

You cannot select records that are not next to one another.

## Select a Field or Fields In a Table

To select a single field, left-click on its name.

To select multiple fields that are next to one another, left-click on the name of the leftmost or rightmost column, hold down the shift key, and then click on the last column at the other end of the range you want to select.

To unselect the columns if you've chosen multiple columns click on the column name for a column you didn't select or click on one of the cells in the selected range.

You can't select multiple columns that aren't next to one another.

## Select All Records In a Table

To select all of the records in a table use Ctrl + A.

You can also go to the Find section of the Home tab and choose Select All from the Select dropdown menu.

Or you can click into the top left corner of the table in the gray box next to the first field name. (There should be a small barely visible gray arrow pointing at the table data in the bottom half of that gray box.)

When all of the data in a table is selected the cells with data in them are highlighted blue and the field names are highlighted in a darker gray color.

## Delete a Field From a Table

To delete a field/column from a table, right-click on its name to see the columns/fields dropdown menu, and choose Delete Field.

You can also select the column by left-clicking on its name, and then use the Delete option in the Records section of the Home tab or use the Delete option in the Add & Delete section of the Fields tab under Table Tools.

Whichever option you choose, Access will ask if you're sure you want to delete the selected records. Say yes if you are.

You cannot undo deleting a field.

## Cut a Record or Records From a Table

If instead of deleting a record from a table you want to remove the record(s) from the table but have it available to paste into a different table, you can Cut the record(s).

For a single record, right-click on the gray box at the left-hand side of the row you want and choose Cut from the dropdown menu.

Or you can also select the record(s) you want and then use Ctrl + X to cut. Or select them and use the Cut option in the Clipboard section of the Home tab.

Whichever way you do it, Access will present you with a dialogue box asking if you want to delete the record(s). Choose Yes if you want to proceed and the record(s) will be removed from the table.

In the case of cutting a record or records, the information is not actually deleted at that point. You can paste it back into the existing table or a new table as a new record(s) using Paste Append from the Home tab.

(You can also paste the data over an existing record or records using Ctrl + V or right-click and Paste from the dropdown, but that overwrites the information in an existing record or records. Ctrl + V and right-click to Paste don't seem to work for a brand-new record. To use them to insert a brand-new record it looks like you'd need to start that record and then paste over what you started.)

If you do cut and paste-append a record in the same table and there is an ID column, that pasted record will have a new ID value. Even though it's the same information Access will treat it like a new record. So don't cut or delete information from a table if that matters to you.

## Copy a Record or Records From a Table

To leave a current record or records where they are but take a copy to paste elsewhere, highlight the record(s) and then either use Ctrl + C or use the Copy option in the Clipboard section of the Home tab. For a single record you can also right-click and choose Copy.

Keep in mind that for any copied record that has an ID value that ID value will change when the record is copied elsewhere.

## Paste a Record or Records Into a Table

To paste a record or records you copied or cut into a table go to the Clipboard section of the Home tab and click on the arrow under Paste. Select the Paste Append option. This will add the record(s) to the bottom of the table.

You can also start a record by entering something in the first available field so that an ID is assigned and then either right-click on the gray box for the record and choose Paste from the dropdown menu or select the record and then use Ctrl + V.

Be careful when pasting into a new table that it makes sense to do so. Access will paste in as much of your information as it can as long as the data types of the fields match, but Access doesn't have any way to evaluate the appropriateness of what you're pasting in beyond a match to the field data type. So if you have a Short Text field Access would let you paste in an entry that had a value of 100 even if every other entry in that field for a thousand rows had been a customer name.

\* \* \*

Okay. I wanted to insert a little break here because I'm going to now cover how to copy, cut, and paste fields, but I honestly wouldn't normally do that in Access. Databases aren't really geared towards that sort of thing. Access can do it, but if you're really going to be moving around a bunch of columns in your tables, I'd personally do so in Excel and then upload to a new table.

## Cut a Field From a Table

To cut a field from a table, highlight the column by left-clicking on its name and then choose Cut from the Clipboard section of the Home tab. (Cut is not an option in the dropdown menu for columns.) You can also highlight the column and then use Ctrl + X.

## Copy a Field From a Table

To leave a current column of data where it is but take a copy of the column to paste elsewhere, highlight the column by left-clicking on its name, and then either (a) right-click and choose Copy, (b) use Ctrl + C, or (c) use the Copy option in the Clipboard section of the Home tab.

## Paste Data Into a Field In a Table

If you're overwriting data in an existing column, then copy or cut and paste are pretty simple. You just left-click to highlight the column where you want to paste your copied or cut data and then either (a) right-click and choose Paste, (b) use Ctrl + V, or (c) use the Paste option from the Clipboard section of the Home tab.

But when you've cut or copied data and are trying to put it into a new column, you have to create that column first. Only then you can paste your data into that newly created column.

Note that the column name will not copy over, just the data.

# Formatting Options For Tables or Queries

Okay, so that was how to amend records in a table in Access. You can do most of those same things in a basic query as well but I wouldn't recommend that you do so. Make it a habit to edit your data in your tables and forms. Use the queries to pull in that information and display it. If you want to amend what a query displays, do so through the Design View which we'll discuss soon.

First, though, I do want to cover some basic formatting options that you can use for either a table or a query.

## Change the Height of Your Rows

If you want to change the height of a row, you are going to have to change the height of all the rows in that table or query. You can't change just one.

To do so, there a couple options.

You can hold your mouse over the line between two rows until the cursor turns into a line with an arrow pointing upward and an arrow pointing downward, and then left-click and drag to your desired row height.

You can also right-click on a row and then choose Row Height from the dropdown menu. At that point you can either enter a desired value for the height or click the box for standard height to revert your row back to the standard row height used by Access.

Finally, you can go to the Records section of the Home tab, click on the arrow under More, and choose Row Height from there which will also bring up the Row Height dialogue box.

Once you change a row height you cannot use Ctrl + Z to undo it.

## Change the Width of a Field

To change the width of a field/column, you can hold your mouse over the line between that column and the one to its right until the cursor turns into a line with an arrow pointing to the left and an arrow pointing to the right. Left-click and drag to your desired column width. (Note that I was not able to use Undo to reverse this after I did it.)

You can also right-click on the column name and then choose Field Width from the dropdown menu to bring up the Column Width dialogue box. (Yes, it really does work that way.) From there you can enter the value you want or click the box to change the width to the standard column width. You also have a Best Fit option which will try to set the width of the field to the best choice given the field name and data entries for the field.

Finally, you can go to the Records section of the Home tab, click on the arrow under More, and choose Field Width from there to bring up the Column Width dialogue box.

Unlike with rows where changing the height of one row changes them all whether you have them selected or not, with columns only those that were selected will change. And if you use the Best Fit option each of your selected columns will change to the width that's best for it.

## Hide a Field

You can hide a field or fields by right-clicking on the top of the selected columns and choosing Hide Fields from the dropdown menu.

You can also do so by selecting the column(s) you want to hide and then going to the Records section of the Home tab, clicking on the More dropdown arrow, and choosing Hide Fields from there.

## Unhide a Field

To unhide a previously hidden field or fields, right-click on the top of any column and choose Unhide Fields from the dropdown menu. This will bring up the Unhide Columns dialogue box. Any field name that isn't checked is currently hidden. Place a check in the box for any field you want displayed.

You can also at the same time remove the check from any box to hide a field/column that's currently visible so this is also another option for hiding a field.

The Unhide Fields option is also available from the More dropdown menu in the Records section of the Home tab.

## Freeze Fields

If you have a table where not all columns of data are visible on the screen, you may find yourself wanting to make sure that certain columns stay visible as you scroll to the right to see the rest of your data.

To "freeze" the column(s) you want to keep visible, select the column(s), right-click, and choose Freeze Fields from the dropdown menu. The columns/fields you chose to freeze will move to the left-hand side of the table and will remain visible as you scroll to the right.

You can freeze columns one at a time or as a group. If you freeze them one at a time, the order in which you freeze the columns will impact the order in which they are displayed.

Another way to freeze your fields/columns is to select the fields, go to the Records section of the Home tab, click on the arrow under More, and choose Freeze Fields from the dropdown menu there.

While I like Freeze Fields, you do need to be careful in using it because if you later choose to unfreeze your columns, that new column order will remain. If you're going to be uploading additional data to a table from an external source I would suggest that you not use the Freeze Fields option on that table.

## Unfreeze Fields

To unfreeze your fields/columns, simply right-click on any column name in the table and choose Unfreeze All Fields from the dropdown menu. There is not an option to unfreeze one field at a time.

You can also go to the Records section of the Home tab, click on the arrow under More, and choose Unfreeze All Fields from there. With this option you can be clicked anywhere in the table, you don't have to right-click on a column header first.

# Queries: Basic Detail Query

Now that you know how to create and work with tables, let's discuss how to create queries.

The most basic type of query involves a single data source (either a data table or a query) and pulls in information from that source without attempting to further summarize or analyze that information. This is the type of query where you can still amend a record and have it impact the underlying data table.

The reason you might create a query like this is to, for example, pull in only a subset of the columns/fields from the original source.

You could also combine this type of query with criteria that narrow down the results to just a subset of the records in the original table. For example, all customer transactions from 2019 only.

For all queries, I use the Query Wizard.

(From here on out I'm just going to talk about doing this with a table as the source, but it can be done with another query as well.)

We'll start with this simple type and then we'll work our way up to more complex types later. This is the most basic form of what's called a Select Query.

Okay. Let's create one.

First, click on the table you want to use to build your query.

Then go to the Queries section of the Create tab and click on the Query Wizard. This will bring up a New Query dialogue box.

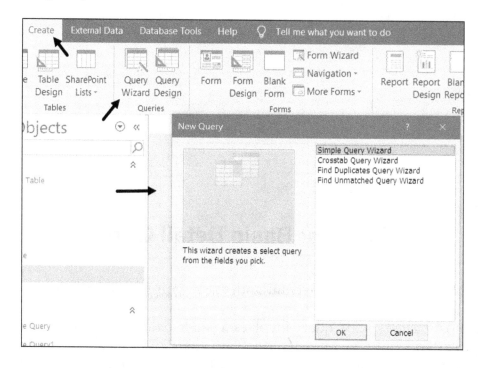

For this type of query you want to choose the Simple Query Wizard. (In this book that's the only type of query we're going to cover.)

Click on that query type and then click on OK. This is what you'll see.

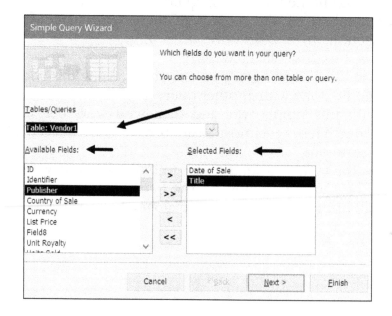

The dropdown menu on the left-hand side should show the table you clicked on before you opened the Query Wizard. If not, you can use the dropdown to change your table selection.

The dropdown lists all of your data tables and queries with all tables listed first followed by all queries. Each table has Table before it and each query has Query before it, regardless of the name you used.

Below that on the left-hand side is a listing of Available Fields from the table/query that's shown in the dropdown.

The right-hand side which shows your Selected Fields will be blank when you start because you haven't yet selected any fields to include in your query.

If you want all of the fields from your chosen data source, you can use the double right-hand arrow in between the Available Fields and Selected Fields boxes.

If you just want specific fields like I chose above, then click on the name of each field you want, in the order you want them, and use the single right-hand arrow.

As you select fields, they will move from the Available Fields list to the Selected Fields list.

If you decide that you don't want the fields you've selected, you can remove all selected fields by using the double left-hand arrow or you can remove a single field by clicking on its name and then using the single left-hand arrow.

Once you've selected the fields you want, click Next.

You will now have the choice of whether the query should be a Detail query or a Summary query.

Because in this instance we just want to bring over our data as it exists now, we're going to leave Detail selected. (We'll walk through a Summary query in a minute.)

For now, click Next.

The next screen will give you an opportunity to rename the query to something useful to you. Otherwise it will take the name of the table it was derived from and add query on the end. To change that name, click into the white box and enter the name you want.

(If you don't change the name here, you can always change it later by right-clicking on the name in the All Access Objects pane and choosing Rename from the dropdown menu.)

Leave "Open the Query to View Information" checked so that you can see your data when you're done.

Click on Finish.

You should now see a new query on the left-hand side in your All Access Objects pane and it should also open in your main workspace with the columns/fields you selected.

Because we didn't impose any additional criteria or try to place a summary on the data, it should be the exact same number of rows as the source data table.

Also, because there's nothing to distinguish this query from the source table, you can actually edit it like you would a table. Any edits made will be reflected in that original table, but like I said before, I don't recommend doing that.

# Queries: Basic Summary Query

Alright, now let's create a Summary Query. We're still only working with one table here, but this time we're going to get Access to summarize our data for us.

This is the data we're working with:

| ID | Date of Sale | Identifier | Title | Publisher | Units Sold | Total Royalty |
|---|---|---|---|---|---|---|
| 6 | 8/1/2017 | 123456789 | A Title | An Author | 1 | 1.25 |
| 7 | 8/2/2017 | 123456789 | A Title | An Author | 1 | 1.25 |
| 8 | 8/3/2017 | 123456789 | A Title | An Author | 1 | 1.25 |
| 9 | 8/6/2017 | 123456789 | A Title | An Author | 1 | 1.25 |
| 10 | 8/10/2017 | 123456789 | A Title | An Author | 1 | 1.25 |
| 11 | 8/1/2017 | 34567892 | Another Title | An Author | 1 | 2.32 |
| 12 | 8/2/2017 | 435671 | A Third Title | An Author | 1 | 3.14 |
| 13 | 8/3/2017 | 123456789 | A Title | An Author | 1 | 1.25 |
| 14 | 8/6/2017 | 34567892 | Another Title | An Author | 1 | 2.32 |
| 15 | 8/10/2017 | 34567892 | Another Title | An Author | 1 | 2.32 |
| 16 | 8/1/2017 | 34567892 | Another Title | An Author | 1 | 2.32 |
| 17 | 8/2/2017 | 34567892 | Another Title | An Author | 1 | 2.32 |
| 18 | 8/3/2017 | 34567892 | Another Title | An Author | 1 | 2.32 |
| 19 | 8/6/2017 | 435671 | A Third Title | An Author | 1 | 3.14 |
| 20 | 8/10/2017 | 435671 | A Third Title | An Author | 1 | 3.14 |

Note that we have entries for three different titles in this table. I want to generate a report that gives me the same information as this report, but I want it grouped by title. Which means I can either group on Identifier or Title because in this case they are unique and tied together.

To start with, I do the same as before. I click on my table in the All Access Objects pane and then go to the Create tab and choose Query Wizard from the Queries section.

From there I choose Simple Query Wizard and click on OK.

In the next screen I'm going to choose the four data fields that I want to use, Identifier, Title, Units Sold, and Total Royalty.

Here we go:

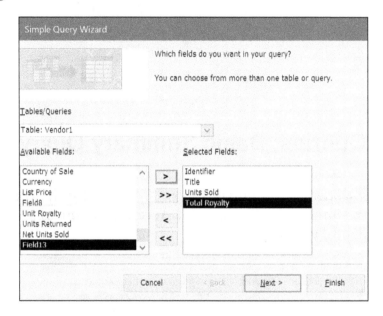

Once I have my fields, I click on Next and get this dialogue box:

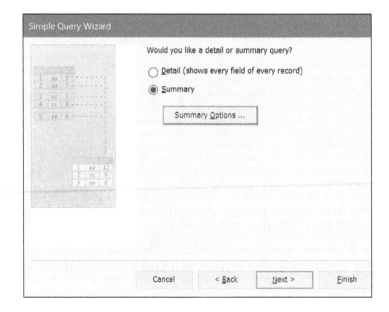

This is where things deviate from the Basic Detail Query. Now we click on "Summary" instead and then click on the gray button that says Summary Options.

This brings up a separate dialogue box called Summary Options. That box lists each selected field that looks like it can be treated as a number and gives the option of calculating the Sum, Average, Minimum, or Maximum for each of those numbers.

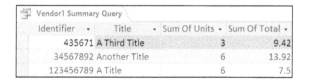

In this case I want to Sum both the Units Sold and the Total Royalty so I check that box for each one and then choose OK.

From there it's the same as before. The next screen is where you can change the name of the query and choose Finish.

This is what the result looks like because we wanted summary data and not detail data:

| Identifier | Title | Sum Of Units | Sum Of Total |
|---|---|---|---|
| 435671 | A Third Title | 3 | 9.42 |
| 34567892 | Another Title | 6 | 13.92 |
| 123456789 | A Title | 6 | 7.5 |

(Note that the totals in this query result are not going to match the totals in our last example because we were using different source data.)

Since this is a summary query, instead of my original ten detailed entries, I now have just three rows of data, one per title/identifier, and the values shown in the next two columns are total units and total royalties for each of those titles.

A basic summary query like this can be very handy when you have a lot of individual entries and you want to see results at a higher level.

Since with this type of query there is no longer a one-to-one tie between the original source table and the query, you can't modify these results from within the query. The option to add or delete a record is grayed out and you can't edit any of the entries. If there was an edit to the data that needed to be made, you'd have to do that in the original source table or related form.

(Which is why I encourage you to get in the habit of doing so even when there are queries that can be modified.)

# Query Views and the Design View

This is a good point in time to stop and talk about your available query views now that we have a query that's doing more than just showing information from a data table.

To change your view, go to the Views section of the Home tab, click on the arrow under View, and choose the view you want.

You have three choices.

The one we've been using, Datasheet View, shows your actual results. This is the default view.

The next one, the SQL View, is one you aren't going to use at this level of knowledge. It basically lets you use SQL to create a query. Unless you're already familiar with SQL, you're probably just going to leave that alone.

(Although in *Access 2019 Intermediate* I will show you how to use what's stored there to create a basic Union Query which has to be done using the SQL view.)

The final view, Design View, allows you to make edits to your query. This is one I use often. Let's look at the query we just created in Design view:

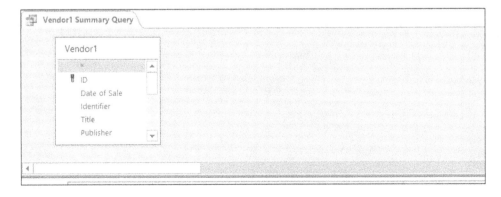

The top half of the display shows you the tables that you're currently using for that query. In this case, we just had the one so that's all that shows. (We'll walk through an example with multiple tables in a minute.)

For each table, you'll see a box with the name of the table (in this case, Vendor1) and then the available fields for that table.

The * at the very top allows you to add all of the fields to your query at once rather than have to add each individual one. There's a scroll bar on the right-hand side because this table has more fields than are currently visible.

If you ever open a query in Design View and don't see the top section, it's just because the field selection area is taking up the whole space. It's not because it's not there. To fix this, hold your cursor over the gray bar right under the tab with the query name and right above the field listings (which we'll describe below) until your cursor looks like a bar with arrows pointing upward and downward. (You may just have to click on the line to get the cursor to look that way.)

Once it does, left click and drag downward until you can see the gray area with your queries and tables showing. Also note that if you have to make this change it will be considered a change to the design of the query and you'll want to save when you exit or you'll have to do it again next time you open that query in Design View.

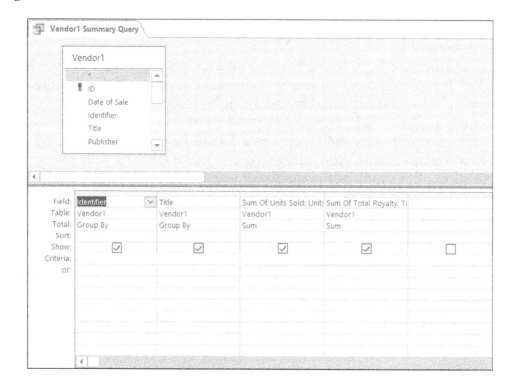

The bottom half of the Design View display shows which fields have been selected for inclusion in the current query and how they're being used.

The first row in that bottom section lists the field/column name. Note that the name Access assigns to those second two columns has been changed. Since we're summing the values it names those columns "Sum of [X]" where X is the original column name.

If you want to change the field name, replace the text to the left of the colon. For example, right now it says "Sum of Units Sold: Units Sold". If I wanted that to be Units Sold, I could rewrite it as "Units Sold: Units Sold". You have to keep the :Units Sold portion because that's the name of the original source field/column.

If I wanted to rename the Identifier field which is currently listed as "Identifier" I'd also need to add a colon. So I could write "ID:Identifier" and then the column would display as ID instead of Identifier. Here's both columns renamed as seen in Datasheet View:

| ID | Title | Units Sold | Sum Of Total |
|---|---|---|---|
| 435671 | A Third Title | 3 | 9.42 |
| 34567892 | Another Title | 6 | 13.92 |
| 123456789 | A Title | 6 | 7.5 |

Going back to Design View, the second row in the bottom section is the name of the query or table that field is being pulled from. Since we're just working with one table here, that's the only option. If there were more than one table this would be a dropdown that listed all available tables and queries.

The third row is how that field is being used. In this case we have two fields that are being used to Group our data, Identifier and Title, and two fields that are being used to create summed values.

In this example our results only had three rows because the Identifier and Title fields were identical. But if they weren't, then our data would be summarized by each unique combination of Identifier and Title.

Like here where I've changed the title for a few rows for Identifier 123456789 to A Title Revised. Now we have two rows for that identifier, one for each title associated with it.

| ID | Title | Units Sold | Sum Of Total |
|---|---|---|---|
| 435671 | A Third Title | 3 | 9.42 |
| 34567892 | Another Title | 6 | 13.92 |
| 123456789 | A Title | 4 | 5 |
| 123456789 | A Title Revised | 2 | 2.5 |

This is a good time to point out that queries are dynamic. If you change the data in a data table that is feeding a query, the next time you open that query it will reflect those changes. Usually you don't even have to close the data table for the changes to carry through although I have at least one data table where it seems I do have to close it first.

Also, if you're in Datasheet View for a query when you change the underlying data table you will have to Refresh from the Records section of the Home tab before that open query shows the changes. But in this case I was in Design View so as soon as I switched over to Datasheet View I could see the changes.

Okay. Back to our walkthrough of Design View.

In addition to Group and Sum there are many other options available for how to use a field such as Avg which takes an Average, Min which returns the minimum value, Max which returns the maximum value. etc.

In general I use Group, Sum, Min, Max, and Expression. (Expression is for when you build a formula to make a calculation. That's covered in *Access 2019 Intermediate*.)

Below that is a row where you can specify how to sort the data in the query. It's a dropdown menu with Ascending, Descending, and not sorted as the available options. (I never use it. If I'm going to sort a query, which I sometimes do, I do it from the Datasheet View.)

The next row after that is a check box so that you can specify whether to include that field/column in Datasheet View. (You may at some point in time want to use a field to select certain data but then not have that field display in your query. I think I've only ever needed to do that once, but it's there if you need it.)

Finally, there's a section where you can add Criteria to apply to your field when creating the query. For example, you could specify that only values greater than zero be included or that only customers in Colorado be included. This is where you'd do that or where that would show. (We'll cover the basics of Criteria later.)

Also, when you have the Design View open there may be a Property Sheet pane visible on the right-hand side of the screen. If it isn't visible, go to the Query Tools Design tab and click on Property Sheet in the Show/Hide section.

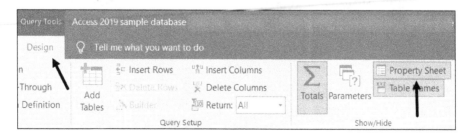

This will bring up the Property Sheet which looks like this:

This gives you the ability to specify a Description, Format, Input Mask, or Caption for each field. For numeric fields you also have a Decimal Places option.

There are two main reasons I use the Property Sheet.

The first is to apply a format to my numbered data. So, for example, in this query the third column is royalties which is a currency amount.

I select my column by clicking on the top gray bar so that it's highlighted black and then go to the Format option of the Property Sheet and click into the box that shows the current format. That will display a dropdown arrow which I then click on to show a list of available formats where I click on Currency from the dropdown menu.

Next, I go to the Decimal Places field and bring up that dropdown menu to choose two decimal places.

(The Decimal Places field is very useful when you have data that has a lot of decimal places in it and where you don't care about the value to that level of precision and don't want that column to be incredibly wide. If you don't limit the number of decimal places your value will show in Datasheet View as a series of pound signs #########.)

The second reason I use the Property Sheet is to change the displayed column name for summed values.

As I mentioned above, when you summarize data in Access it by default shows it as Sum of [X] where X is the field you were summarizing. So here we have Sum of Units Sold and Sum of Total Royalty when I'd rather the columns were labeled Units Sold and Royalty.

We already changed the name of the Units Sold column in the field name. Doing it that way means that the field name used by other queries that reference this query will be able to use Units Sold instead of Sum of Units Sold. This can be very helpful because if you don't do that you can end up with a query that has a field called Sum of Sum of Sum of Units Sold.

But if all you care about is the current query and making your column names more user-friendly, then the Caption option will do that for you. Here I've applied a caption to the Total Royalty column as well as changed the number format to Currency with 2 decimal places.

Whichever way you use to change the column name, it will look the same in Datasheet View as you can see here where I used Units Sold: Units Sold for the third column and where I used the Property Sheet caption option to show Royalty for the fourth column.

| ID | Title | Units Sold | Royalty |
|---|---|---|---|
| 435671 | A Third Title | 3 | $9.42 |
| 34567892 | Another Title | 6 | $13.92 |
| 123456789 | A Title | 4 | $5.00 |
| 123456789 | A Title Revised | 2 | $2.50 |

When I was writing the original version of these books, I did go through my own database and change the field names rather than using the caption field which is what I'd done previously. That was in Access 2013, but I noted that there were three situations where Access did not automatically carry through my change to the field name and it appears that it still works the same in Access 2019.

One is when I used that field in a calculation in the same table where I changed the field name.

If you change the name before you build a calculation and haven't saved the changes to the query yet, the expression builder will show the old name. If you then build an expression it won't work until you close the query, save the changes, and reopen the query.

If you build an expression and then change the name of a field used in that expression, you will need to edit the expression to use the new name.

The second was in a report. The report updated to show the values in detail cells fine, but it did not update the summary rows.

The third was in some of my union queries where I hadn't copied and pasted the SQL language direct from the source query but had instead written the SQL language myself using the old field/column names.

Bottom line: While permanently changing the name of a query field certainly makes it more intelligible and easier to use for other queries or reports, if you're dealing with an active Access database you need to go through and make sure that you haven't broken any queries or reports when you do so.

A good indicator that you broke something is if you get an unexpected Enter Parameter Value dialogue box the next time you open a query or report.

\* \* \*

Okay, so those are your various views and what they contain. Keep in mind that if you make formatting changes or make any name or criteria changes in your query in Design View that when you close the query Access will ask if you want to save your changes to the design of the query. If you want to keep those changes you made, you need to say Yes.

Unlike changes to data which save automatically, any changes to formatting or query criteria must in fact be saved.

# Relationships

Next we're going to explore how to link data from two separate tables or queries to create a query that combines information from both of them. But first we need to discuss relationships, because if you don't tell Access how your tables and queries are related, you can't pull information from more than one at a time.

This is a snapshot of some of the relationships that exist in my current Access database:

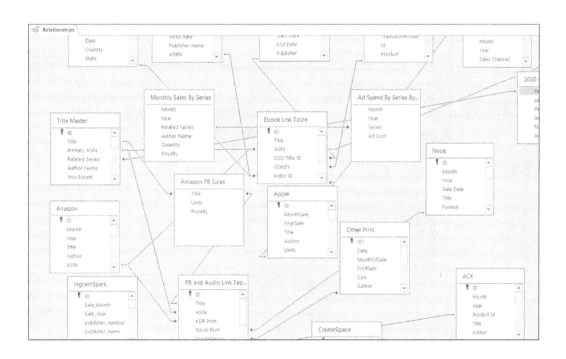

It looks insane, right? I mean, there are lines going every which way. But keep in mind this is something that has built up one relationship at a time over years.

It looks so involved because for almost every query I create—and I have over a hundred of them—I have to have relationships established between the tables and queries I'm going to use in order to create that query.

But when you're just starting out it is much, much simpler.

Let's walk through how to do this.

Before we even go to the Relationships view, you first have to know if there are any ways to link your tables or queries. I mentioned before that I receive a lot of vendor reports for the same books but that they all have different identifiers in those reports. Title A can be 12345 with the first vendor and AX2132 with the next. And vendors list my title names differently, too, so I can't directly link title to title across those reports.

What I've had to do is create a separate table in my Access database that lists the title of each of my books and the identifier that each vendor uses so that I can then link sales of Title A across vendors using that "anchor" or master table.

If the data you're working with doesn't naturally have a field that can be linked across your data tables, you may have to create something like that as well. Ask yourself, how do I know that this record in this table is related to this other record in this other table? What is it that ties the two together? And is it unique enough to use? That's the field you'll use to build your relationships in Access.

Okay, then. I'm going to assume you know what field you're using to link your tables or queries and proceed from there.

First, go to the Database Tools tab and click on Relationships from the Relationships section.

In my test database even though I hadn't created any links there were three linked tables already showing related to MSysNavPaneGroups. If that happens to you, right-click and choose Show Table from the dropdown menu to see a list of your available tables and queries.

This will bring up the Show Table dialogue box.

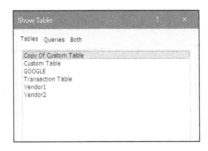

Select the tables or queries you want to link and choose Add. (To select more than one table at a time, use Ctrl before you click on the second one, or you can add them individually.)

When you're done adding the tables or queries you want, close the dialogue box. The tables or queries you selected should now be visible.

If you realize after you close the dialogue box that you actually wanted to add another table or query, you can right-click in the workspace and choose Show Table from the dropdown menu to bring it back.

At this point there is not a relationship between the tables or queries you've selected. Access doesn't know how they relate to one another. They're just sitting there.

In my database, Access added my two tables right into the middle of those other three mystery tables, so the first thing I did was left-click on each of the tables I'm working with and drag them to some open space.

In this sample here I've chosen a Title Master table that I created with summary information for my titles and a vendor table called Vendor1.

This is a pretty typical example where one or two fields might overlap between the tables or queries but the rest of the table or query will contain unique information. (Otherwise, why have two tables or queries.)

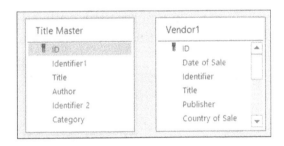

We need to link these tables. In this case, we're going to link Identifier1 in the Table Master to Identifier in the Vendor1 table.

So first what I need to do is left-click on the field name (Identifier1) that I want to use from the first table. And then I'm going to hold down that left-click and drag over to the field I want to link to in the second table.

Sometimes it's really hard to actually drag over to the field you want to use (especially in Design View for a query), but fortunately in the Relationships screen you don't have to get it perfect. If you drag to the wrong field you can just fix it in the Edit Relationships dialogue box which will appear as soon as you create a link between the two tables/queries.

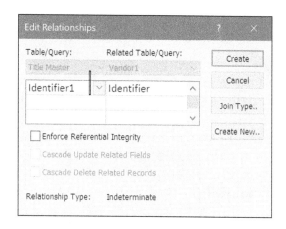

What you're seeing here is a listing of the two fields you're going to use to create a relationship. On the left-hand side will be the field name for the table you started with. On the right-hand side will be the field name for the table you dragged to.

If one of the fields is not the correct one, click on its name and you should see a dropdown arrow appear. Click on that arrow and select the field you do want to use from the dropdown. It should be every field available in that table or query.

(You can't change the tables/queries that you're using, so if that part is wrong you need to cancel and do it again.)

Next, you need to specify the join type, so click on Join Type on the right-hand side and tell Access what kind of join this is. You have three options.

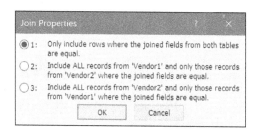

You can specify that only information is included when both tables have entries for that join field. (One that I rarely use because if I were pulling together sales from multiple vendors that would drop out any book that didn't sell on every vendor which I don't want to risk doing.)

The other two options let you specify that Access always include entries from one of the tables and then pull in data from the second table as it matches.

Which table you choose as your base table will depend on what you want to see.

For example, here I'm trying to establish a relationship between my master table and vendor table. If I include all records from my master table and then pull in matching results from the vendor table I'll have blank entries for every title that didn't have a sale on that vendor.

If I instead use the vendor table as my base, I'll only show titles that sold on that vendor and no other titles.

Which option I choose comes down to what I'm using the query for. If I want a report of my audiobook sales, for example, and I know it's a final query that I'm not going to do anything else with, then I'll use the vendor report as my base because only about 10% of my titles are in audio so that gets rid of a lot of blank lines I don't need.

But if I'm going to take that audio query and later use it to join up with paperback, video, and ebook sales, then maybe I want to use the title master instead.

Basically, experiment and figure out what gives you the result you want to see. I normally default to have the Title Master be the base data table for a join with my own database.

Okay.

Once you've selected your join type, click on OK, and then click Create in the Edit Relationships dialogue box.

(I tend not to click the box to enforce referential integrity because the way I work in my database means I won't always have referential integrity. What enforcing referential integrity does is makes sure that you never have orphaned data. So, for example, if you're using Customer ID, that you never have an entry in your transactions data table with a Customer ID that's not in your customer data table. But because I sometimes have situations where I published a new title and don't yet know what ID a given vendor is going to assign to that title until after it sells, I encounter situations where my report would "break" if I enforced referential integrity. I catch these situations with a set of checks and balances that compare the sum of my sales from each vendor report to my total sales report. If I've just uploaded a new vendor report and my total sales report is $5.32 less than the sum of the individual sales reports then I know I have a book or books that earned me $5.32 during the month where I haven't yet recorded that vendor ID in my master title table for that format.)

Once you've established a relationship between your two tables or queries, you should see that they are now joined by a line that connects the two fields you used to link the data tables or queries.

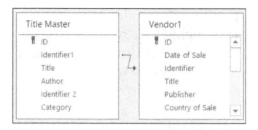

You can double-click on that line at any time to bring up the Edit Relationships dialogue box. You can also click on that line and use the Delete key to delete the relationship, although I'd be careful about doing so because it may impact queries you've created that are based on that relationship.

Once you have all of your relationships built, click on Close under the Design tab, and say yes to saving your changes when asked.

You are now ready to build a query that links data across those two tables or queries, so let's do that next.

# Queries: Queries Using More Than One Table or Query

First, if you try to create a query using the Query Wizard and more than one table or query and you haven't established a relationship between the two tables or queries, you will get an error message halfway through the process. If that happens, click OK, go create the relationship (as discussed in the prior chapter) and come back to the wizard after you've done so.

Second, know that sometimes you have to build up to the query you want to create. You can't always build the query you want right away.

For example, I have a report that shows total sales by type (print, ebook, audio, and video) for all of my titles. It lists each title, author name, series name, genre, and then units and amount earned by type as well as total units and total amount earned.

When I look at that table in Design View I find that it was created using my Title Master table and one query each for my ebook sales, print sales, audio, and video sales.

Looking at just the ebook sales query shows that it was created from a report of ebook sales by month which itself was created from twelve separate queries, one for each ebook vendor.

It's possible that someone who was really good at Access or computer programming might be able to build that report with fewer steps, but it's pretty common to find help advice on Access when a query isn't working that says you need to use an intermediate query before building the one you're trying to build.

And what I've found for myself in Access is that I often need to walk my way to the report I want step-by-step by building various queries that roll my data up to higher and higher levels before I can combine the results effectively.

Alright. Let's build a query now that uses multiple tables or queries. In this case we'll use two tables, but it could be any combination of tables and queries and would work the same.

First, go to the Create tab and choose the Query Wizard from the Queries section.

This is still a simple query, so choose the Simple Query Wizard.

Next, select the first table or query that has fields you want to include in your query. In this case we're going to use Title Master and choose the Title, Author, and Category fields.

After you've selected all the fields you want from the first table or query, change the dropdown menu to the other table or query you want to use. In this case that would be Vendor1 for me. Now select the fields you want from that table. I'm going to choose Units Sold and Total Royalty.

I try to select my fields in order, so sometimes that means I switch back and forth between the tables and queries I want to use so that I can select the fields in the "correct" order.

This is what I ended up with:

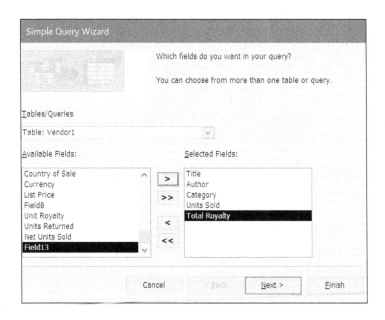

You can't tell that the fields came from two sources, but they did.

I should also note here that I didn't include the Identifier field that linked the two. Just because it's the field being used to link the two tables together doesn't mean it has to be part of the query.

When you're done, click Next.

If all you wanted to do was pull in the records from the two tables without summarizing anything, you could leave this set to Detail.

In this case, though, I want a summary of units and royalty so I make that choice.

After that I click Next, I leave the query name alone but you could change it if you want, and then I click Finish.

The query should then open in Datasheet View. (If Access tells you it has to open a query you just created in Design View that's a sign that you have an issue somewhere in your query that prevented it from opening in Datasheet view like a type mismatch between linked fields.)

Mine looks like this:

| Title | Author | Category | Sum Of Units | Sum Of Total |
|---|---|---|---|---|
| A Third Title | An Author | Non-Fiction | 3 | 9.42 |
| A Title | An Author | Fiction | 6 | 7.5 |
| Another Title | An Author | Fiction | 6 | 13.92 |

You can see that we've combined fields from two tables into one query, because Category is listed in my Title Master table but Units and Royalty are listed in my Vendor1 table.

The first thing you should do with a new query like this one is check that the results make sense. In this case I had the prior Vendor1 Summary Query that I could compare my results to.

That one had two titles listed for the same Identifier so they're not identical, but when I add the numbers for those two titles together they match to the result for A Title in this query. (By pulling the title field from the Title Master I was able to impose a standardized title onto my results which is something I often need to do with my data since my vendor reports don't do that.)

You can also compare the total values for any numbers you're summarizing to make sure that the totals, in this case, units and royalties, match. (We'll talk about how to pull a quick sum in the next section.)

If things don't match or it doesn't look the way it should, check your join type and check that the fields you've used to join your data were the correct ones. That's usually where the problem will be.

* * *

In the example above we used two data sources, the master table and one vendor table. But you can use more than that. Going back to our classic example in the introduction you could have a product table, a transaction table, a salesperson table, etc. and join all of them together for a query.

When I need to do this, I prefer to have what I think of as an "anchor" table or query. This is a table or query that all of the other tables and queries can tie to. Even if I use five tables to build my query there's one central table that I can anchor them all to. In the example in the last paragraph that would likely be the transaction table which contains an ID for product and an ID for salesperson that lets me link those tables in.

Having an anchor table or query eliminates certain issues you can run into with Access around ambiguous joins or double-counting of results.

Even doing it that way, however, I will sometimes run into an issue with my queries where I tell Access to sum the values but access ends up doing so multiple times. Which means rather than getting an answer of, say 100, I get an answer of 300.

This seems to happen when I'm using a query derived from a query derived from a query. I don't think I've ever had it happen with a query that was derived directly from a data table.

I also want to say it only happens when multiple data sources are involved.

(I've always been able to fix the issue by having my query display the maximum value in the field rather than the sum, so I've never stopped to nail down exactly what causes that to happen. But the fact that this can happen is a good reminder to always check your results.)

# Summary Results, Sorting, and Filtering in a Table or Query

Now let's discuss the various ways you can manipulate and/or evaluate your data directly in a table or query, starting with one of the ones I use most often to check that my results are correct in a query or with a data import, summarizing the results of a field/column.

## Summary Results

I use summary results for units sold and total royalty at each vendor so I can compare those values across all of my vendors to my summary reports to make sure it all matches.

I'll also after I upload new data compare the summary results for the time period I uploaded to the Excel file I used as my source file.

Now, first thing to know is that you have to have the correct data type assigned to a field for this to work. You can only sum the values in a field if the field is a number type of field, such as Number, Large Number, or Currency.

I mention this because you cannot sum numbers that are stored as text and Access will sometimes default to storing numbers as text.

The only option you'll have available if your numbers are stored as text is to count them. And if you figure this out somewhere down the road in a query of a query, often the only way to fix it is to go back to the source data table.

Okay, then. To calculate the sum of the values in a field in a table or query, go to the Records section of the Home tab. There is a Totals option there that has the summation mathematical sign next to it. Click on that. It will add a row at the very bottom of your table or query that is labeled Total on the left-hand side.

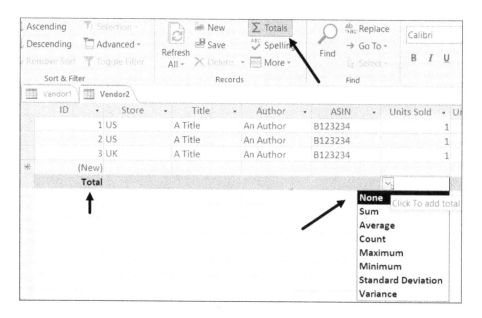

In that row for every single field in that table or query you can now click into the cell for that column/field and there will be a dropdown menu. If the values in that field are considered numbers by Access you will then be able to choose to sum, average, count, take a minimum, take a maximum, calculate the standard deviation, or calculate the variance for the values in that column.

If the values are considered text, your only option is to count the values.

Once you've added a calculation to that row, to remove it, click on the dropdown again and choose None.

I would caution against using any option in that list other than Sum just because there's no way to see that that's what you've done. That row will continue to be labeled Total no matter what choice you make. So you can be taking the average of the values in that column and it will look like you're taking the sum of the values.

To keep the summary row available every time you open that table or query you will need to save changes to the design when you close the table or query. Also, keep in mind that if you do add a summary row to your data table or query that when you export it from Access to Excel that summary row will export as the last row in your data.

## Sorting

When you tell Access to sort your data you are telling it to display your results in a specific order. For example, I often use the Sort function to display my records alphabetically by title or to display them in descending numeric order so that the most profitable titles are listed first.

You can build a sort into a table or query so that the data is already sorted the way you prefer it to be, but inevitably I find myself wanting to sort my data in some other order at some point.

The type of sort available to you is going to depend on the nature of the data in the column you choose to sort by.

Sort A to Z or Sort Z to A is for "text" entries. That means to sort, as it says, alphabetically from A to Z or reverse alphabetically from Z to A. With an A to Z sort, a row with a value of Apples will display before a row with a value of Oranges in the specified column. With a Z to A sort, the row with Oranges would display before the row with Apples.

Sort Oldest to Newest or Sort Newest to Oldest is for date entries. Again, it's just what it says. If you sort Newest to Oldest the record with the most recent date will display first. If you sort Oldest to Newest the record with the oldest date will display first.

Sort Smallest to Largest or Sort Largest to Smallest is for numeric values. And, again, it's pretty straight-forward. If you Sort Smallest to Largest the smallest value will be first. If you sort Largest to Smallest the largest value will be first.

The nice thing about sorting in Access compared to sorting in Excel is that you don't have to worry about selecting the correct range of data before you sort. All entries in a specific row/record stay together no matter what, so you never run the risk of "breaking" your data with a bad sort.

To sort your data, right-click on the column/field you want to use for your sort, and then choose your sort option from the dropdown menu.

If there's already a sort on that column, the chosen type of sort will be highlighted on the left-hand side like so:

See the box around A to Z in that image? That's because the data in question is already sorted on this column using an A to Z sort. You can also see a small little arrow on the right-hand side of the column name that either points upward or downward depending on the direction of the sort.

You can sort on multiple columns this way, but you need to be careful about the order you do the sort in. The last sort you set will be the first way that your data is sorted. So if I want to sort by Date and then within a date by title, I would need to sort the title column first and then the date column.

Another option for sorting your columns is to select the column you want to sort by and then choose Ascending or Descending from the Sort & Filter section of the Home tab.

The Sort & Filter section of the Home tab is also where you can go to remove a sort that you have in place. So if you've sorted your data and now want to return it to its original order, you can go to the Sort & Filter section of the Home tab and click on Remove Sort.

There is an option for an Advanced Sort in the Sort & Filter section, but we're not going to cover it here because it's a little complicated because it uses Design View to build your sort.

## Filtering

Filtering is one I use a lot. And if you're familiar with filtering from Excel then you'll pick it right up because it basically works the same way in Access.

Filtering lets you take your table of data or your query and narrow the results down so that only specific results show. I'll often filter for a specific month and year or for a specific title or a specific series name.

To filter your table, click on the small arrow at the end of the column name. This will bring up the dropdown menu for that column which will include the filter options.

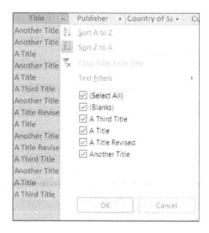

If what you want is a specific value, then click on the box next to Select All. This will unselect all values. And then click on the box next to the value you do want and click OK. That will narrow down the data displayed to just the rows/records that match the value in the box you checked.

You can also check multiple boxes to see multiple results. For example, I'll often use the checkboxes to quickly see the results for a set of titles that are all related but not in the same series.

Sometimes, though, you'll want to filter based on a set of criteria instead. I, for example, often have to filter based on the presence of the text "overdrive" in book titles for one of my vendors.

To do that, depending on the type of data you're dealing with, you'll click on the small arrow at the end of the column name to bring up the dropdown menu and then place your cursor over either Date Filters, Number Filters, or Text Filters as the case may be.

For the example we're looking at it would be Text Filters.

This will display a secondary dropdown menu off to the side of the original dropdown menu, such as this one:

The exact options listed will vary depending on whether you're dealing with a date, a number, or text.

From there, choose the filter type you want. When I'm looking for titles that have "overdrive" in them I choose the Contains option which will look for the word overdrive anywhere in the text of each entry, for example.

Equals has to be an exact match. Does Not Equal has to not be an exact match. Begins With has to start with that value. Does Not Begin With must not start with that value. Does Not Contain will return entries that don't contain that value anywhere in them. Ends With must end with that value. And Does Not End With must not end with the value.

Whichever one you choose, Access will then display a Custom Filter dialogue box where you type the criteria it needs to use. For text the value is not case-sensitive so Overdrive and overdrive are treated the same.

Another way to access the Filter dropdown menu is by clicking on Filter in the Sort & Filter section of the Home tab. It's only an available option if you're clicked into a single cell of your data table or have selected a single column. Clicking on the Filter option will open the dropdown menu in the table for that column just like right-clicking does.

To remove a filter you already applied, you can click on the filter symbol on the right-hand side of the column name to bring up the filter dropdown menu and then choose "Clear Filter from [Field]" where [Field] is the column name. That will remove the filter for that one column.

To temporarily remove all filters from your table or query, you can click on the Filtered option at the bottom of the data table.

(This is also an easy place to check to see if your table is currently filtered. If it says Filtered, it is. If it says Unfiltered or No Filter, it isn't.)

Clicking on that option only temporarily removes the filter. You can click on Unfiltered in the exact same spot to put the filter(s) back.

To permanently remove all filters from the table, go to the Sort & Filter section of the Home tab, click on the arrow under Advanced, and choose Clear All Filters from the dropdown menu.

* * *

One final note about sorting or filtering in Access. When you sort or filter a table or query, even if you then return the table or query to its original appearance, when you go to close that table or query Access will ask, "Do you want to save changes to the design of [X]?"

Note that this is not asking you about saving changes to your data. The minute you change a data entry in a table or query, that change has been saved. This is just about changing the sort order or keeping a filter on your data or keeping a new column order. Usually my answer on this is "No" unless I was deliberately working to change the appearance of that table or query.

# Queries: Using Simple Criteria to Narrow Down Results

Okay. Next.

There are going to be times when you want to build a query that doesn't just summarize the results from other tables or queries, but actually only displays a subset of those results.

For example, I don't want to include in my units sold numbers any books that I've given away for free because I don't consider those sales.

Also, I have a number of reports I've written that pull in just the current year's values. I don't want my sales data for 2013 to 2021, I just want to see 2021 values.

To do this, you can use the Criteria row in the Design View for the query in question.

Build your query like you normally would using the Query Wizard and then you can make your edits in Design View. Access has a help topic called *Examples of Query Criteria* that covers the various options you have, but let me go over a few of the most common ones here.

Here is an example of a query I use that contains two text-based criteria.

| ASIN | Units: Net Units Sold | Royalty: Est USD Royalty | Transaction Type |
|---|---|---|---|
| Amazon | Amazon | Amazon | Amazon |
| Group By | Sum | Sum | Where |
| ☑ | ☑ | ☑ | ☐ |
| Like "B*" | | | Not Like "*KENP*" And Not Like "*KOLL*" And Not Like "*Free*" |

That first column there is using the criteria,

Like "B*"

That's saying to include any entry that starts with a capital B.

The last column is using the criteria,

Not Like "*KENP*" And Not Like "*KOLL*" and Not Like "*Free*"

That's saying to exclude any entry that contains either KENP, KOLL, or Free anywhere in that cell.

You'll notice a couple things with both of these examples. First, the text I'm referring to is in quotes. You have to always include text in quotes. Second, I'm using what's called a wildcard when I use the asterisk (*). An asterisk stands for any number of characters. When I write B* that means B1, B12, B123, B1234, etc. where those numbers could be any letter or number or a space.

In the *KENP* example, that's saying KENP with any number of characters before or after it.

If I had instead used B? that would represent one single character so it would mean B1 but not B12, B123, or B, for example. You can use multiple question marks together, so if you know the results you want are four characters long but nothing else about them you could use "????" as your criteria.

If you're going to use wildcards, think through how that will work with your data. Sometimes they can have unintended consequences.

Another thing to point out here is that the second example was using multiple criteria for that field. Each one was joined with an AND. So there are three separate criteria being combined there and it works because in that case the criteria used for all three was Not Like so each one eliminated certain entries.

Here is an example of a query that uses number-based criteria instead:

| Field: | Year | Primary ASIN | Title | Related Series | Author Name | Ad Spend: Ad Cost |
|---|---|---|---|---|---|---|
| Table: | Advertising Spend By Ti | Title Master | Title Master | Title Master | Title Master | Advertising Spend By Ti |
| Total: | Group By | Group By | Group By | Group By | Group By | Sum |
| Sort: | | | | | | |
| Show: | ✓ | ✓ | ✓ | ✓ | ✓ | ✓ |
| Criteria: | 2021 | | | | | >0 |
| or: | | | | | | |

The first column, Year, simply says 2021 for the criteria. Because it's a number there's no need for quotes. That's saying only return values that are equal to 2021.

The last column, Ad Spend, has a criteria of >0. Again, no quotes are required because it's numeric. This time it's saying only return values greater than zero.

You can also use the less than operator < and can combine the greater than and less than operators with the equals sign >= and <= to specify values greater than or equal to or less than or equal to.

For multiple criteria you can also use OR which means that the value must meet one of the list of choices.

You can also use NOT followed by a number value to exclude a specific numeric result.

Access has a tendency to modify the criteria you enter to match its display preferences. If you enter "*Excel*" as your criteria, when you go back into Design View you will see that Access has taken your entry and added the word Like at the beginning of it to make:

Like "*Excel*"

In general, when I need to use criteria for a specific purpose I go and look up exactly how to do it rather than try to remember all the different criteria that can be used and how they're written. That help topic in Access is a very good place to start. There are also some great online resources I've found when needed over the years.

# Printing, Forms, and Reports: A Brief Discussion

Okay. So that's the basics of creating data tables and then using queries to combine the information in those tables. That's a lot of what you probably need Access for. The rest, forms and reports, are more the bells and whistles. Nice to have, but not necessarily essential.

But there are going to be times when you want to do more than just look at your data in your Access database and you instead want to print a physical copy of the data or maybe even send a PDF file to someone else.

If you think you will routinely want to do this with the same set of information, then a report is your best bet. A report can be generated from a table, a query, or a form.

To create a basic Report, click on the table, query, or form that you're going to use, go to the Create tab, and click on Report in the Reports section. This will give you a very basic report that has all of the fields from the source table, query, or form.

(You can also use the Report Wizard if you want more control over which fields are included or if you want to include grouping, sorting, or summation values or want to have more control over layout at the report creation stage.)

It's beyond the scope of this book to cover how to then delete fields, format fields, etc. but that can definitely be done and is covered in detail in *Access 2019 Intermediate*. I'll just note here that once you create a basic report you can then work in Design View to turn it into something more customized.

The main issue with working with a report generated with the Report option is that it generally won't print neatly onto a single page. You're very likely to have columns of data that continue on to a second or even a third page.

Another option, and one that I used early on when I was more comfortable in Excel than I was in Access, is to simply export your table or query to Excel and create a formatted document that you can print from there. I personally think that Excel is far more friendly when it comes to printing raw data than Access is. The problem with this approach is if you need to print the date from that same query or table multiple times, because you have to reformat every time.

But the reason using Excel is so nice is because Excel allows you to scale your document to a specified number of pages across or long. Access does not.

In Access the number of pages that your data takes up when it prints is determined by your column widths and the font size of your text. There is no proportional scaling when you go to print to make it fit. Because of that little difference it takes far more time and effort to create a good-looking report in Access than it does in Excel.

That means that for me how often I'll need the report and how heavily customized it needs to be is drives whether I simply export to Excel versus taking the time to create a report in Access.

* * *

To print from Access, open the table, query, form, or report that you want to print, go to File, and choose Print. This will give you the option to Quick Print, Print, or Print Preview. ALWAYS use print preview in Access. You will save yourself a lot of wasted paper by doing so.

When you choose Print Preview it will show how the first page of your document will appear when printed. At the bottom of the screen will be a section that says Page and has arrows.

If your document takes up more than one page, these arrows will let you navigate through each page of your document to see what will print on each page.

I have often in Access found that one column carried over to the next page or, even worse, the edge of a report carried over with no data so that if I were to print right then I'd print pages with just one long line down the edge.

If that happens to you, changing your Page Layout to Landscape may help. If that doesn't work, changing the Margins to Narrow in the Page Size section can also sometimes help.

Other than that, though, you're somewhat limited on your printing options in Access which is why exporting to Excel and printing form there or creating a report become necessary.

If you can get the document looking good enough to print from your print preview, then click on Print in the top left corner to bring up the Print dialogue box. This is where you can specify which pages to print if you don't want them all, the number of copies to print, and, under Properties, that you want to print on both sides of the page.

I often move in and out of the Print Preview when I'm designing a Report because making sure all my columns will fit on a single page is usually the biggest challenge. Always check your header and footer labels as well, because sometimes you reset the column widths but the report will still carry over to another page because of the header or footer.

Okay.

* * *

The one other item we haven't covered yet and are not going to cover in detail but need to touch on is forms. Forms are good for when you want to separate your records into single pages that can be printed one at a time or for when you have a lot of text-based information that you're going to be entering directly into Access or needing to review regularly.

To create a basic form, go to a table or query, click on it, then choose Form from the Forms section of the Create tab. This will create for you a basic form with one page per record.

If you used a data table or a basic detail query to create the form, you can edit the values directly in the form and your changes will carry through to the underlying data table.

If it was a summary query you used to generate the form, you can see the data in the form, but won't be able to edit it.

If you want multiple records to show on a single form page, you can use the More Forms dropdown menu in the Forms section of the Create tab and choose Multiple Items from the dropdown. This will put your records in rows instead of separated onto different pages.

To navigate between pages in a form, use the arrows at the bottom of the workspace. You can further edit your forms in Design View. (This is covered in far more detail in *Access 2019 Intermediate*.)

# Where To Get Additional Information

That's all we're going to cover here. This book was just a beginner guide to Access. It was not by any means meant to be a comprehensive guide. The goal was to make you comfortable with moving around in Access and to give you the ability to work with tables and basic queries.

But Access can do a whole lot more than that.

So where do you go from here?

If you want to continue working with me then your next step should be *Access 2019 Intermediate* which will cover topics like union queries, crosstab queries, and append queries as well as how to customize forms and reports.

But if you just have a specific question you need answered there are a number of other options available to you.

One is the built-in help that's right there in Access.

Often if you hold your mouse over an item, Access will give you a brief description of what it does. Sometimes those descriptions come with a Tell Me More option like the option for Tables in the Create tab.

If you click on that Tell Me More text, it will open for you an Access Help pane covering that specific topic. In this case it opens to a help topic titled *Create a Table and Add Fields*.

Your other option within Access is to go straight to the Access Help screen. You can do this by clicking on the Help tab and then clicking on Help again. This will open an Access Help task pane on the right-hand side of the screen which includes beginner topics as well as a search box.

F1 (if you have your F keys available by default which is not always the case in newer computers) will also open Access Help.

If that's not enough, because sometimes it isn't a question of how something works but can something be done, you can always search online. I recommend including your Access version in your search and seeing if Microsoft support has a solution before you branch out from there.

So search for something like "add fixed value query Access 2019 microsoft support" and then choose the support.microsoft.com or support.office.com result that matches your search.

However, while Microsoft is very good at discussing how things work, they often fail to address what is possible. There are plenty of free forums and websites out there that do cover those kinds of questions, and chances are your question has probably already been asked before. You just need to dig a bit to find it.

Just keep in mind that the internet is full of jerks who sometimes can act very condescending and rude when answering questions, so it's always better in my opinion to find someone else who already asked your question than subject yourself to that. (This is why I usually will try and fail a dozen times on my own rather than go to one of those user boards to see if someone knows the answer already.)

But worst case scenario, you can always ask your question on one of the user forums that are out there. If you do so, just be as precise as possible about what you want to know and be sure to mention the version of Access you're working with and be as clear on your terminology as you can be.

You can also try me. I may already know the answer or be able to find it for you fairly easily. (And if I don't know the answer chances are you'll make me curious enough to go find it.)

Just know that I won't open someone else's Access database so it needs to be a question I can answer without needing to use your database. Just email at mlhumphreywriter@gmail.com and I'll get back to you.

# Conclusion

Alright. So that's it. That's how to approach the basics of Microsoft Access 2019 if you're someone like me who is used to working in Excel but needs an option that lets them combine data in more complicated ways than Excel has historically allowed for.

This book is much longer than the equivalent books I've written for Excel, Word, and PowerPoint simply because Access is much more complex to work with and requires a lot more beginner-level knowledge to work in effectively.

So just a few reminders.

Keep your original data safe somewhere else so that you always have it to go back to. If that isn't possible, be sure to regularly save back-ups of your database.

Work with caution in Access because so many changes that you make in Access are permanent and cannot be undone.

Expect to make mistakes, however. I personally find Access more finicky than Excel which means that on a somewhat regular basis I have to deal with different error messages and troubleshoot them. It's okay if that happens. Google is your friend if you need to understand what a message is telling you or why something didn't look the way it should.

Also, be sure that you have checks and balances in your database or elsewhere that let you confirm that your queries are working. It's somewhat easy with Access to drop data and not know that you have if you aren't doing these types of checks.

Check, verify, and proceed with caution.

But have confidence that you can work through it and make it work. And remember that Access, while intimidating to a new user, is an incredibly powerful tool that is worth mastering.

Good luck!

# Access 2019
# Intermediate
ACCESS ESSENTIALS 2019 BOOK 2

M.L. HUMPHREY

# CONTENTS

# CONTENTS (CONT.)

# Introduction

This book continues from where *Access 2019 Beginner* left off. In *Access 2019 Beginner* we walked through the four main components of an Access database, covered the basics of working within each of those components and in Access in general, discussed how to create a table either from scratch or by uploading an Excel or .csv file, and then covered how to create a basic select query using one or multiple data sources.

But there was a lot that wasn't covered in that book because Access is a very complicated program with a wide range of capabilities. So this book continues where the last one left off.

Here we will cover how to add default values to tables, how to add validation rules to tables, how to add a fixed field to a query, how to add a calculated field to a query, how to create union queries, crosstab queries, and parameter queries, and also how to customize the content and formatting of reports and forms.

That still won't cover all of Access's capabilities, but it will cover everything I've needed to know to use Access to run my small business.

Now keep in mind here that I come to Access as an Excel user who needed more capability than Excel could give me and that from my perspective there are two main reasons to use Access.

One, to create a database that allows you to combine information from different sources into summary reports. (In my case, I have an Access database that combines information from multiple vendors and provides summary reports related to my books and videos.)

Two, when dealing with data that includes entries that contain significant amounts of text. If you're working with those types of entries you'll find that at some point Excel requires manual adjustment of your row height to display the full text of a cell and even then sometimes doesn't do so. Using forms in Access can be a far better solution in that case.

As I mentioned in *Access 2019 Beginner*, I think there are probably far better solutions out there these days for a number of the ways Access may have been used in the past, which means that I probably will not cover in these two books ways to use Access that are of interest to database developers.

For example, I'm not going to cover how to run a delete query, because I think if you need one you need a product other than Access. And I'm not going to dig into how to use SQL in Access at more than a very cursory level of detail. (It comes up with adding a union query, but I suspect there are certain Access users who only use SQL to build their queries and that's not the target audience for this book.)

This book is targeting Excel users who want to be able to learn Access, and is written as a continuation of *Access 2019 Beginner*.

Also, this book is written using Access 2019. The precursor to this book, *Intermediate Access*, was written using Access 2013 and for a more general audience. This book is focused on Access 2019 only.

Honestly, there aren't huge differences between the two—if you've read one you should be able to figure out how to use whichever version of Access you're working in—but I was more careful in the prior book to talk about things like backwards compatibility and how certain options weren't available until certain points in time. Here I'm just assuming you have Access 2019 and don't need to concern yourself with prior versions.

Okay.

So there you have it. I'm going to briefly cover basic terminology and the four components of an Access database again as a review and then we'll dive in on adding default values to a table.

# Basic Terminology Recap

All of these terms were already covered in *Access 2019 Beginner*. I'm going to walk through them again here but in far less detail and without any screenshots.

## Tab

I refer to the menu choices at the top of the screen (File, Home, Create, External Data, Database Tools, etc.) as tabs. Each tab you select will show you different options.

## Click

If I tell you to click on something, that means to use your mouse (or trackpad) to move the cursor over to a specific location and left-click or right-click on the option.

## Left-Click/Right-Click

If you look at your mouse or your trackpad, you generally have two flat buttons to press. One is on the left side, one is on the right. If I say left-click that means to press down on the button on the left. If I say right-click that means press down on the button on the right. If I just say click that generally means to left-click.

# Dropdown Menu

If you right-click on something in Access, for example a field or table name, you will see what I'm going to refer to as a dropdown menu. A dropdown menu provides you a list of choices to select from.

# Dialogue Box

Dialogue boxes are pop-up boxes that cover specialized settings.

# Panes

Panes are task areas that are separate from the main workspace. For example, the All Access Objects pane is on the left-hand side of the workspace by default.

# Scroll Bar

Scroll bars allow you to see your data when there is sufficient data to take up more space than is currently available on the screen. They are visible on the right-hand side or bottom of the pane, workspace, or dropdown menu when needed.

# Arrow

If I ever tell you to arrow to the left or right or up or down, that just means use your arrow keys that point in that direction.

# Tab Through or Tab To

I may instead tell you to tab through or tab to your data. This is different from the tabs we discussed above. In this instance, we're talking about using the Tab key to move right or the Shift and Tab key together to move left.

# Table

There are actually two different types of tables I talk about in Access.

One is one of the four main components of an Access database where your imported or input data is stored.

The other is how data appears in Datasheet View for both tables and queries.

# Column/Field

Every table in Access consists of rows and columns of information. Columns, which can also be referred to as fields, run across the top of the workspace and are named Field1, Field2, etc. by default.

# Row/Record

Rows/records run downward in a data table.

You should think of each row of a data table in Access as containing a related set of information that will always stay together. Technically, this is best referred to as a record.

# Cell or Entry or Value

When I refer to a cell in Access I am referring to the intersection of a column and row.

It is probably more appropriate to refer to values or entries, but in a generic sense I will still say something like, "click into the cell next to the cell that contains the value you want to copy."

# Control Shortcuts

In Access there are various control shortcuts that you can use to perform tasks like save, copy, cut, and paste.

Each time I refer to one it will be written as Ctrl + a capital letter, such as Ctrl + C which will copy a selection and means to hold down the Ctrl key and the c key at the same time.

# Undo

Access does have an Undo option which will generally let you undo your last action. It's available in the Quick Access Toolbar in the top left corner of the screen or by using Ctrl + Z. But don't rely on it. Not everything in Access can be undone.

# Overview of the Four Main Components of an Access Database

As discussed in *Access 2019 Beginner*, I break Access down into four main components: Tables, Queries, Forms, and Reports. Each component (object type) is shown by default in its own section in the All Access Objects pane.

## Tables

Tables are the bedrock upon which everything else is built. This is where all of your data is actually kept.

It is up to the user(s) of the Access database to define what columns of data are in each table and provide the values that go into each record.

## Queries

Queries are where you tell Access how to pull together the information in your various data tables or from other queries. They are where the bulk of the analysis is done. Your tables are the raw material, your queries are where you put that material together to make something useful.

## Forms

Forms allow you to display each record from a table in a more user-friendly way. If you're doing direct data entry into your Access database (something I would caution against), they can be easier to work in than tables. An edit to an entry in a form is recorded in its associated table.

# Reports

Reports take the information you have in a table or query and they put it in a report format that has better formatting for print or distribution.

# Tables: Default Values

Okay, now that we've reviewed the basics from *Access 2019 Beginner*, let's talk about how to use default values in tables.

I don't use default values in my Access databases because I usually upload all of the information in my tables from other sources. But if you are entering data directly into Access you may want to set a field to a default value.

I would only do this if you have fields in your table that are 95% of the time a single value. So, for me for example, if I had a field that said whether an item was a book, an audiobook, a video, or a template I might set that to book as a default because the large majority of what I publish are books.

Let's walk through how to do this.

Open in Design View the table with the field where you want to set a default value.

Click on the field name in the top portion of the screen. For this example I've clicked on a field called YearSale that is formatted as a Number.

Now, look in the Field Properties section at the bottom of the screen.

|  | Field Properties |
|---|---|
| General  Lookup | |
| Field Size | Long Integer |
| Format | |
| Decimal Places | Auto |
| Input Mask | |
| Caption | |
| Default Value | 0 |
| Validation Rule | |
| Validation Text | |
| Required | No |
| Indexed | No |
| Text Align | General |

About five lines down you should see a line that says "Default Value". Enter there the default value that you want for that field.

Keep in mind that the default value must match the field data type. For example, you can't set a default value of "fifty" in a field that has a data type of Number. (If you do that, Access will assume you're trying to reference the value in another field and will put it in brackets and then generate an error message when you try to return to Datasheet View.)

Also, you can't set a default value for any primary key field or the Access ID field since those have to be unique values.

After you've set your default value, save your changes to the table with Ctrl + S or by clicking on the save icon in the Quick Access Toolbar in the top left corner.

Return to Datasheet View. (If you forgot to save, Access will prompt you to save the changes to the table. Say Yes.)

Here I've entered a default value of 2021 for the YearSale field and you can see that for a new record that value is already populated:

| ID | Purchase Am | YearSale | Click to Add |
|---|---|---|---|
| 521865984 | | | |
| 1063737268 | $0 | | |
| 1727406757 | $0 | | |
| 1822708994 | $500 | | |
| 1856010266 | $1 | | |
| 1942142299 | $100 | | |
| (New) | $0 | 2021 | |

This was a new field that I just added to a table that already had six records in it. Note that Access did not add the default value to those existing records. This only applies to new records from the point where I added the default value.

Default values do not have to be fixed values.

Typing Date() into the field will provide today's date.

Typing =Date()+10 will give a date ten days from now. Etc.

Also, if you're using text for your default value you should put quotation marks around the text, especially if there is any sort of punctuation involved. This lets Access know it's a fixed text entry and not a field reference. So, "January" would put January into each new record for that field. (If you don't use quotes, Access will add them for you.)

That's default values. Now on to data validation.

# Tables: Validation Rules

Another trick to use in Access if you're inputting data is to include a validation rule for a field. Access automatically runs certain validation rules against input values based on the field type. So you can't enter "fifty" for a Number field, for example. It will also convert 1.2345 to 1 in a Number field set to Integer.

But you still may want to add further constraints to a field.

For example, maybe in my YearSale field I know that the only valid values are from 2013 to 2120. (I don't expect to still be alive and making entries to an Access database in a hundred years, but that makes sure I'm not going to bump up against my validation rule anytime soon. I just want to prevent those times when I try to enter 1920 or 20201 accidentally.)

To add a validation rule to a field, open your table and go to Design View.

In the top section, click on the field where you want to add validation, and then go down to the Field Properties section at the bottom.

About the sixth row down will be for Validation Rule which is where you enter your criteria. Below that will be the row for Validation Text where you enter an error message that will appear when someone enters the wrong value.

| | Field Properties | |
|---|---|---|
| General Lookup | | |
| Field Size | Long Integer | |
| Format | | |
| Decimal Places | Auto | |
| Input Mask | | |
| Caption | | |
| Default Value | 0 | |
| Validation Rule | >2012 And <2121 | ← |
| Validation Text | Enter a year of sale that is between 2013 and 2120. | ← |
| Required | No | |
| Indexed | No | |
| Text Align | General | |

Above I've written a rule for a number field where the value must be greater than 2012 and less than 2121. If someone enters a value outside of that range they see an error message that tells them to, "Enter a year of sale that is between 2013 and 2120".

If you're familiar with Excel, the way to write a rule is basically the same as how you'd write a formula in Excel. You can use the numeric operators (>, <, <>, =, etc.) as well as AND and OR. You can also use wildcard characters for text like the asterisk (*) and the question mark (?).

(Just be careful if you're using AND that you don't set criteria that are mutually exclusive so make it impossible to enter any value. If I did >1999 AND <2000 and I'm only allowing whole numbers in that field, there's nothing that would satisfy both.)

As with default values, you will need to save your changes before you can return to Datasheet View.

Also, when you do that, Access is going to tell you that your data integrity rules have been changed and will ask you to confirm that you really wanted to do that. It will also ask you whether you want it to run the rules against your old data.

Ideally, the answer there is yes that you do want to run the rules against your old data because why have rules in place if they don't apply to part of your data. However, if you already have a lot of values in your table that can take a significant amount of time.

If you do have an entry in your existing table that doesn't fit your validation rule, Access will tell you that existing data violates the new setting and ask if you want to keep going.

If you say yes to continuing, Access will still keep that old value in the table and won't flag that record for you in any way. You'll just know that it exists somewhere in your table.

\* \* \*

Once you're back in Datasheet View, if you have a validation rule in place and you enter a value that doesn't work, Access will show an error dialogue box with the message you provided under Validation Text. You will need to change the value until it does meet your rule or delete the value.

Here is an example of an error dialogue box using the Validation Text I entered above:

This is why providing a clear explanation of what's required in your Validation Text is so necessary.

\* \* \*

Another sort of validation is to require that a field be completed for any new record. To do this, go to the Design View, click on that field, and in the Field Properties section change the value next to Required (which should be directly under Validation Text) to Yes.

# Queries: Include a Fixed Value in a Query

Now let's talk about how to include a fixed value in a query.

One of my summary queries in my Access database is a union query, which we'll discuss in a minute. It takes all of my ebook sales from all of my different platforms and combines them into one single query.

When I built that query I didn't want to lose who the original vendor was for each of my sales. I still wanted to be able to look at the final query and ask, "How much have I made from ebook sales on Apple for this title?" or "On Google?"

Each of my queries that ties to a vendor table is named with that vendor name, so I can always open the original queries to see those values. But I wanted to have a column in my final query that showed the vendor name so that I could just go to that one query and filter on that vendor name and have my answer.

To do that, I had to add a new column/field that would list the vendor name as a fixed value.

I originally learned how to do this in SQL View. (For those who know SQL, you basically add a new field to the SELECT portion of the query. Put the value you want to repeat in single quotes, follow that with AS, and follow that with the field name you want. So, 'Nook' AS Vendor, will give you a field labeled Vendor where all entries are Nook.)

But after I learned how to do it in SQL View, I realized that it was incredibly easy to do in Design View. So that's the method I'm going to teach you here. All you need is the column/field name you want to use and the value you want to show in that column/field.

First, open your query and go to Design View.

Next, go to the next available field in the bottom section where you can see your selected columns, and in the top row type the following: your chosen field name, a colon, and then in single quotes the value you want shown in each entry for that column.

So,

Vendor: 'Vendor1'

for example.

Here is a query in Design View where I have added a second column to include a field name Vendor with a value of "Vendor1":

Here's how that looks in Datasheet View:

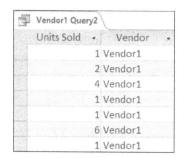

There you have it. It's that easy to add a column with a fixed value to a query. Just name, colon, and then single quotes around the value you want for text. (If you want a fixed number value, just type the number value, no need for the single quotes.)

And, of course, be sure to save the changes to your query when you close the query since this is considered a design change that must be saved to stick.

# Queries: Write a Simple Calculation into a Query

Now let's discuss how to include a calculation in a query.

I tend to use the Builder which is located under the Query Setup section of the Design tab under Query Tools when you have a query open in Design View.

But the reason I'm covering this now is that you really don't have to do that. You can actually write your formula right there under Field Name. And it's not that different from including a fixed value.

The only difference is that you reference other field names instead of fixed text, and use basic notation to indicate addition, subtraction, multiplication, and division.

A plus sign (+) stands for add. A minus sign (–) stands for subtract. An asterisk (*) stands for multiply. And a forward slash (/) stands for divide.

(If you know how to write formulas in Excel, it's basically the same.)

To reference field names, if the field name is all one word, you can just write it out. But if the field name has spaces in it, you need to use brackets around the name.

So, the field name Title can be left as Title, but the field name Total Royalty needs to be written as [Total Royalty].

Let's do an example. I have a query that includes fields for Units and Total Royalty and I want to calculate the average royalty per sale which we can get by taking Total Royalty and dividing it by Units.

To do this, I'm going to go to the first free column in the field listing in Design View and I'm going to type in

Royalty Per Unit: [Total Royalty]/Units

and then on the third row I'll change the dropdown menu to Expression. While I'm at it, I'll use the Property Sheet to format the field as Currency.

The portion of the text on the left-hand side of the colon is the field name I want to use, in this case Royalty Per Unit.

The portion of the text on the right-hand side of the colon is my expression/ equation. In this case, the field Total Royalty divided by Units. I've put brackets around Total Royalty since there is a space in the field name. I could just as easily put brackets around Units, but I don't have to.

So here it is in Design View. I've scrolled over until the field was the only one visible:

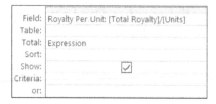

And here's what that field included in my data table in Datasheet View looks like:

| Title | Author | Category | Units | Total Royalty | Royalty Per Unit |
|---|---|---|---|---|---|
| A Third Title | An Author | Non-Fiction | 13 | $9.42 | $0.72 |
| A Title | An Author | Fiction | 12 | $7.50 | $0.63 |
| Another Title | An Author | Fiction | 23 | $13.92 | $0.61 |
| Total | | | | | |

I now have my new column, Royalty Per Unit, in my query and it's calculating the value for each row by taking the total royalty and dividing it by the total units for that row.

Simple enough.

\* \* \*

But it can be more complicated than that, especially when dealing with a query that uses multiple tables or queries for its data.

Let's now walk through an example that uses a text "calculation" instead and also uses a field that occurs in two different tables that are feeding into the query.

What we're going to do is create a field called Title by Author. And it is going to consist of three parts, the Title as provided in the Title Master table, the fixed text, " by ", and then the Author name which is also coming from the Title

Master table but which we don't have to link to that table because it's a field that only occurs in the Title Master table.

Here's a quick visual of the two source table fields and the expression we need to use:

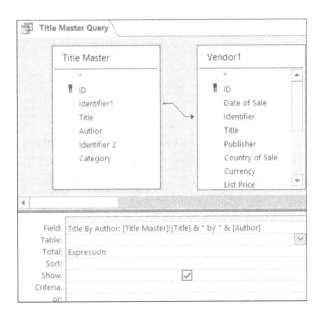

Once more, this works much like it would with writing a formula in Excel. To separate different text entries we use the ampersand (&) and quotation marks around any fixed text.

What we end up with is:

Title By Author: [Title Master]![Title] & " by " & [Author]

That's saying, create a field with the name Title By Author. Create that field by taking the Title value from the Title Master table (the table name is followed by the exclamation mark and then you list the field name), join that to the text that consists of a space, the word by, and another space. And then join that to the value in the field Author.

Since Author only occurs in the Title Master table we don't have to list the table name. If you tried that with Title, there would be an error message when you tried to go back to Datasheet View that said that Title could refer to more than one field.

When working with text like we are here, you have to tell Access every single space or punctuation mark you want to use. If you don't, it will just smoosh all of your different text fields together. So that " by " portion is necessary and needs to have those spaces included on both sides for the final value to display properly.

And here's our result:

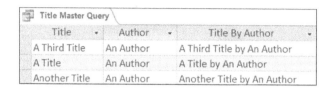

You can see that the third column is called Title By Author and that it includes the value from the Title column joined to the value from the Author column for each row with a space, the word by, and another space.

* * *

Okay.

That's how you can simply type in an expression for a new field in a query in the Design View.

But when I'm writing more complex equations, I prefer to use the Builder instead, so let's walk through how to do that now.

First, open your query in Design View and click into the Field row of a blank column.

Next click on Builder which looks like a little magic wand and is located in the Query Setup section of the Design tab under Query Tools.

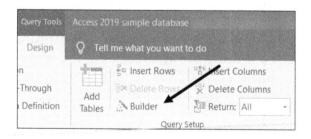

This will bring up the Expression Builder dialogue box:

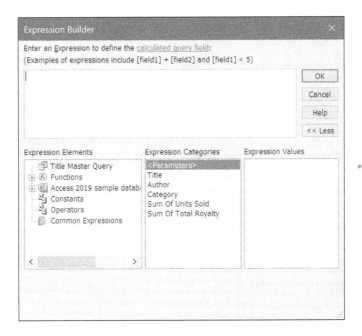

The white space at the top is where you build your equation.

Expression Elements, in the bottom section on the left-hand side, allows you to navigate to any field in a table or query. It also shows folders for your expression building elements such as Functions, Constants, and Operators.

It should default to having your current query listed at top and selected.

Expression Categories in the center shows the fields that are available to you based upon your Expression Elements selection. So by default it will list the fields in your current query.

If you have not saved the query since you added a calculated field, then those new calculated fields will not show here. Also, if you've changed a field name and didn't yet save, it won't show as changed yet either. (So maybe save before using the Builder if you've been doing that sort of thing.)

Expression Values shows more detailed options when they exist. It generally doesn't show anything useful unless you've chosen Functions, Constants, Operators, or Common Expressions in the Expression Elements section.

While you're looking at your fields in your current query it will just be blank or show <Value>.

* * *

Going back to Expression Elements.

If you click on the plus sign next to your database name, which is generally the third item listed, you'll be able to see all of your Access object types. Clicking on the plus sign next to an object type (e.g., table) will show all of your objects of that type that currently exist in the database. Clicking on the name of one of those will show you the fields available from that object in Expression Categories.

When working on a query that involves more than one table or query as its source, selecting your fields through the database navigation option makes sure that the table name is properly referenced in your formula.

If you just select your fields from your table as they're listed in the default view in the Builder they'll be added in without the table/query reference, which may be an issue.

For example, here, I've selected the Title field from my default listing when I opened the Builder, but selected the Author field after navigating to Tables, Title Master, and choosing the field that way.

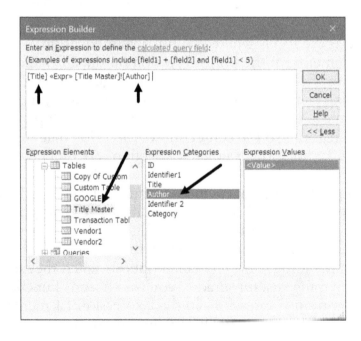

(Both fields were selected by double-clicking on them in the Expression Categories section.)

What's showing in that white space is gibberish right now, but I want you to notice that for the Title field it's listed as [Title] but that for the Author field it's listed as [Title Master]![Author]. They both came from the same table. They both could have been written with or without the table name included. The reason one was written one way and the other was written the other way just comes down to where I selected the field name from.

If you're working with a query that has multiple tables and queries feeding into it, I suggest playing it safe and choosing your fields for your expression through the database navigation option so that your table name is always included for you automatically.

* * *

Okay. Now let's revisit the Expression Categories and Values sections again.

When you're dealing with a query, table, form, or report Expression Categories is just going to show field names.

But it can also be used to show categories of functions, operators, and constants that will then be listed individually in the Expression Values section. This lets you add Operators like *, /, +, etc., Constants like False, Null, True, or Functions to your expression. Just double-click on it.

I don't do it that way because I'm familiar enough with what I need (+, -, etc.) and I keep things pretty simple so I just type it in up above. But it can be a good place to look if you're trying to figure out if something is available to you in Access.

* * *

Alright, so now let's build an expression or calculation.

Let's build the one we did before which was Total Royalty divided by Units, both of which are fields in my current query.

I'm going to do that by selecting my Total Royalty field first.

Because both of my fields are in my query, I can just use the default field listing that I see when I open Builder.

I double-click on Total Royalty in the Expression Categories section so that it's added into the white space above.

Next, I type a forward slash which indicates division.

After that I double-click on my Units field name from the Expression Categories listing.

And that's it. Here it is, ready to go.

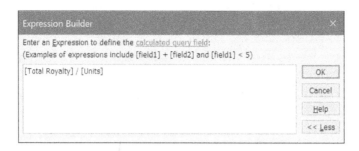

I click on OK and it's added as a field in my query, still showing in Design View.

Now, because I didn't take any time to name my calculation it will appear as Expr1: and then my calculation. You need to either change that Expr1 to what you want that field to be called or add a Caption in the Property Sheet to change how that field name is displayed or it will also show in your table as Expr1.

Alright, now let's go back and build our text-based calculation that combined Title and Author.

I click into an empty field in my Design View and open the Builder once more.

I can't build this one the same way as the last because of that Title field I'm using. Access doesn't know which Title field I want. To clear away that ambiguity, I need the table name.

I can either navigate to the table I'm using in this query and double-click the field name from there to make Access add the table name. (So click on the plus sign next to the database name, then click on the plus sign for tables, and then click on my table that I'm pulling that field from, and double-click on the field I want.)

OR I can just type in the table name myself once I've added the field into the white space. It all kind of comes down to how much I remember in that particular moment how to list out a table name in an expression.

You can technically write the entire expression in the builder by hand without ever clicking on a field name or operator if you really want to. At the end of the day what matters is that you have all the components in place.

So for our text-based one I used the navigation to the table option which means both of my fields end up with a table name. Here it is:

Since this is my second unnamed expression I've built, Access calls it Expr2.

When you first build an expression using Builder it will show a category of Group By in the third row. You don't always have to, but I'd recommend changing that to Expression.

(When I didn't do so on these two, they both worked, but the Total Royalty/ Units calculation threw up an input box that wanted me to provide a value for units which I simply ignored by closing it. Ideally, you don't have pop up boxes like that showing up because they indicate something's not quite right somewhere. Unless you intended to have an input box, of course, but I usually don't.)

* * *

Alright. So those were pretty simple examples which you could build either way.

Here is an example of a more complex formula to show why it's easier to work in the Builder rather than directly in a field:

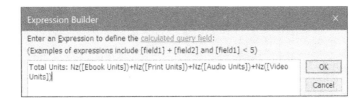

The formula there is:

$$\text{Total Units: Nz([Ebook Units])+Nz([Print Units])+Nz([Audio Units])+Nz([Video Units])}$$

In this example, I'm adding the values from four separate columns in the query together, one each for ebook, print, audio, and video sales. Even though it's just addition, it's far easier to see and write the formula in the Expression Builder, especially since before I learned to rename my field names some of those were SumOfSumOfSumOfUnits.

Alright. Now let's talk about troubleshooting some issues with expressions because you're probably wondering about that Nz I've included around each entry in that formula.

# Queries: Troubleshoot Issues with Expressions

If you look at the screenshot above you'll see that I've placed an Nz() around each of the values I want to add together. The equation I used is:

$$Nz([Ebook\ Units]) + Nz([Print\ Units]) + Nz([Audio\ Units]) + Nz([Video\ Units])$$

The reason I did that is because I found when I was first building my database that when I tried to add multiple items together that Access wouldn't return a result for a specific record unless it had a value for each of the items I was trying to add.

So in the example above where I want the total number of units for a title that have been sold in ebook, print, audio, and video I would have to have had at least one ebook sale, one print sale, one audio sale, and one video sale for Access to return a value.

Problem is, I put titles into audio OR video. So I'm never going to have a title that is both in audio and in video.

The use of the Nz() around each value lets Access still add the results from the other categories without being stopped by the fact that there's a null value for one of my categories.

Now, you may not have this issue, depending on how your data is set up. For example, I have this issue with respect to my video units which show blank lines when there hasn't been a sale of that title, but not with respect to my audio units which show a value of zero when there hasn't been a sale. So you can also get around this by making sure that there are values of zero in all of your entries instead of null values. But for me, using Nz( ) was the easiest fix.

M.L. Humphrey

* * *

Another issue you may encounter is the Enter Parameter Value dialogue box which I mentioned I was seeing above for Units.

We'll talk later about how to deliberately generate one of these dialogue boxes, because you can create a query that relies on user input and this box is how to get that input, but as I mentioned above, I had it show up when my field wasn't categorized as an Expression field.

I also often see them when I have an imperfect field reference somewhere.

Basically, Access is looking for a value in a field and can't find that field for some reason, so asks the user to provide it.

For example, when I was writing the original *Access for Beginners* I decided to rename all of my fields to get rid of that "Sum of Sum of Net Units Sold" that Access likes to create.

I replaced all of those field names with more sensible names like "Units".

But that broke some of my reports which were still trying to find values using the old field names. (This happened in the summary rows in my reports. The detailed data fields were fine but any field that summed those values had to be replaced.) The way I knew the report had been broken was when I saw one of these Enter Parameter Values dialogue boxes appear after I opened the report.

If that happens and it's down to a field name, open the query or report that is requesting that parameter in Design View. Next, figure out where a field with that name is being used. So above you can see that it says Enter Parameter Va… and right below that it shows the field name, Units.

Replace that field name with the correct one. This may require you to go back to another table or query to fix the issue.

For example, if I have a query that pulls in results from another query, then even odds are that the field name that isn't working is in that original query not my new one.

For me with my reports when I changed the field names and this happened, I had to delete the summary fields and regenerate them.

Bottom line on this one, if you see one of these boxes and aren't expecting it, your query or report is pointing to something that doesn't exist and you should fix that.

(I will note here that I have had queries that generate correct results even with one of these boxes popping up. I'd just hit enter when I saw it each time and everything still worked, but better to fix the issue.)

\* \* \*

That brings up something I touched on briefly in *Access 2019 Beginner* but want to touch on again here.

As we covered there, you can designate a field name using the colon. So Units: Sum of Units Sold will name a field Units.

Access is pretty good at carrying through that change to other queries or reports.

If, however, you already used that field in an expression in that specific query before you made the name change, then when you change the name and try to go to Datasheet View, Access will generate an error message that you have an expression with invalid syntax.

It also won't let you close the query without fixing the issue. You will need to either change the field name back or go fix all references to that field name in any expressions in your current query.

\* \* \*

Another time I've seen that invalid syntax error message appear is when I was editing an expression that I'd written in Access and I accidentally dropped a paren or a bracket. If Access can figure out that you dropped a bracket it will tell you, but for complex equations it just knows that things don't match up.

So if you were working on an expression right before this error appeared, go back and walk through your formula and confirm that all opening parens have a matching closing paren and that all opening brackets have a matching closing bracket.

\* \* \*

Another one I mentioned briefly in *Access 2019 Beginner* is that I have on occasion run into situations where Access was double-counting or even triple-counting a value when I combined multiple tables or queries. One solution I've found that works in those scenarios has been to change the option in the Total row in

Design View from Sum to Max. This may not work all the time, but it's worth trying and has always been easier for me to do than try to figure out what's causing it.

\* \* \*

Another I've run into when trying to build an expression was if there were two or more tables involved that used the same field name. For example, Title. In that case you need to make sure that you're specifying which table to pull that field from.

You can write it like the example in the last chapter where we had:

[Title Master]![Title]

Where the [Title Master]! portion was referencing the table where the field is located.

Your other option if you don't want to remember how to do that is to go into the Builder and select your fields from the Expression Elements section after navigating to your table or query via the database listing.

\* \* \*

One final issue to be aware of is, of course, relationships. If you're pulling data from more than one table or query and you haven't established a relationship between those tables/queries that will generate an error message. Access doesn't know how to link various sources of information unless you tell it how to do so.

Also keep an eye out for inappropriate relationships where you've told Access to link tables or queries in a way that doesn't make sense. And for issues with the join type where the results that display aren't all the records you thought you should see.

Ambiguous joins generally appear when you have multiple tables or queries and Access can't tell how A links to B links to C. I usually solve this with an anchor or master table/query which links A directly to both B and C.

\* \* \*

You will probably run into other errors along the way.

My advice is to step back and think about what you were doing right before you saw the error and then go through step-by-step to make sure everything is working the way you think it should.

Check for parens, brackets, colons, etc. and make sure they're all in the right place.

If you typed in field names, check that they're correct.

Make sure your data types are the right ones for that type of expression.

And make sure the operators (+, -, etc.) that you use are correct.

And always, always double-check your results at the end and ask if they make sense.

Also, when working in Design View know that some errors will not register as errors until you move back into Datasheet View. So I would recommend if you're building multiple expressions to finish an expression and then go to Datasheet View to confirm it works before moving on to your next expression. That at least helps to narrow down the issue to that one expression.

# Queries: A SQL Crash Course

Next I want to talk about Union Queries, but in order to do that we need to take a quick crash course in SQL. Basically, everything we've been doing so far has been working with a pretty little interface that makes what's really going on user-friendly to people like me who aren't computer programmers and don't want to work directly in SQL to make things happen.

But behind the scenes, all of those queries we're building are being run with SQL, which is a programming language that's pretty common.

For every query you build there is a corresponding SQL statement. To see that statement, simply choose SQL View from the View dropdown when you're in a query.

You'll see something like this for a basic select query that's not doing any summations and just pulling in data from four fields:

Or something like this for a more complex query that is only pulling in values over zero and is taking the sum of units and revenue:

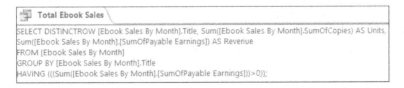

Let's take a quick step back and talk about what that SQL View is doing. That first image above is of a SQL statement for a query with four columns of data pulled from a single data source.

What that text says is:

SELECT Vendor1.[Date of Sale], Vendor1.Title, Vendor1.Publisher, Vendor1.[Units Sold]

FROM Vendor1;

Let's break that down.

The first word, SELECT, is telling Access to go get certain information.

The next part, Vendor1.[Date of Sale], is saying to go to the table named Vendor1 and pull in the field named Date of Sale.

Then we have, Vendor1.Title which is doing the exact same thing except asking for the field named Title. (Remember that we don't need brackets when dealing with a single word.)

After that it's the same thing to pull Publisher and Units Sold.

Next we tell Access where to pull it from using the FROM clause. So, in this case, from Vendor1.

The wording above is how Access wrote the query when I used the Query Wizard to create that query. But because this is a query that pulls from one table, it would work just as well without the Vendor1 portions of the SELECT line.

You could write

SELECT [Date of Sale], Title, Publisher, [Units Sold]

FROM Vendor1;

and get the same result.

Okay.

So getting back to understanding this. What the SQL View is doing is showing you the computer language that is visually represented in the Design View. But the SQL View is the actual instructions. The Design View is just a pretty interface that makes it easier for people like me to work in Access without having to learn SQL.

Let's now walk through that more complex query. Here it is:

SELECT DISTINCTROW [Ebook Sales By Month].Title, Sum([Ebook Sales By Month].SumOfCopies) AS Units, Sum([Ebook Sales By Month].[SumOfPayable Earnings]) AS Revenue

FROM [Ebook Sales By Month]

GROUP BY [Ebook Sales By Month].Title

HAVING (((Sum([Ebook Sales By Month].[SumOfPayable Earnings]))>0));

We already talked about SELECT. That's the first step. So Access is being told to go select those fields from the Ebook Sales By Month query.

But this time it's DISTINCTROW which means we're grouping our data. You can see in the GROUP BY section that we're grouping on Title. So there's going to be one row per title.

There are also some summary calculations that we've told Access to perform since we're only going to have one row per title. You can see that in the SELECT section where the field names are surrounded by SUM ( ) for Copies and Earnings.

Also, the AS is telling Access to change the name of the fields to Units and Revenue so that we don't get back a hot mess of SumOfSumOfCopies.

Finally, there's the HAVING clause which says only bring in records where the sum of Payable Earnings is greater than zero.

And then, so SQL can know it's done, the query ends with a semi-colon (;).

* * *

Kinda crazy, huh? If it's the first time you've run across SQL that probably felt like drinking from a firehose. And you can forget most of it.

Because the key pieces of information you need to take away from everything we just discussed is:

That the SELECT portion of a query is where you tell Access what fields to include in the query. The order you list them in is the order in which they'll appear in your data table.

And that for any query you can copy that language from the SQL view and it will recreate the query wherever you paste that information.

Also that using a semi-colon tells Access to stop so you only want one of those and you want it at the end.

$* * *$

There is far more to SQL than what we just covered. Microsoft has some good overviews on their website and I'd suspect that a lot of programmer-types probably work almost exclusively in SQL when they work with Access, but for our purposes this is where we'll stop.

# Queries: Union Queries

Okay, then. Now let's take that minimal SQL knowledge and use it to build a union query.

First, let me walk through why I use them.

I decided I wanted to know what my total sales were across all of my different vendors. At the time the only way I could think to combine my reports from each vendor was using something called an Append Query.

With an Append Query, you basically run that type of query and it adds (or appends) your data onto the end of a data table you've established for that purpose. It worked fine, but the problem was that I had to run each append query for each vendor separately each month.

So every month I was having to sit there and run twelve different queries to get my information.

It was very time-consuming. And when I found sales that were missing from one of my vendors, I had to rerun the whole thing. (Until I figured out how to add a fixed variable and then I just had to rerun the query for the vendor with the missing info.)

I've said it before, I'll say it again, I basically learn how to do things in programs when I get too annoyed with the current way I'm doing them. I don't learn everything up front, I just learn what I need until I figure out I need more.

So after about a year of this, I went in search of a different solution and discovered the beauty of union queries.

All I had to do with a union query was create it once and I had my data combined into one report just like that.

I love union queries. They are wonderful. Which is why I'm going to teach them to you.

## M.L. Humphrey

So. What exactly does a union query do?

It essentially takes the results from various queries and stacks them on top of each other. Even better, the queries that you stack don't have to be tied to one another by any sort of relationship.

Ideally, what you should have is the same information in the same order in each one so that it makes sense to stack the results, but that's not even required. You could stack completely unrelated data into the same report. All it would need to do is probably be the same data type and use the same number of columns.

Now, the trick to union queries is that they're built using SQL. There is no Design View.

(But, hey, maybe someday developer guys? A little click and drag interface? Better than rearranging where you go to import Excel files for no apparent reason? Just saying.)

Anyway. Back to union queries.

One of my union queries is Ebook Sales By Month. It contains fields for Month, Year, Title, Identifier, Units, Revenue, and Platform. And it pulls this information in from twelve different sources. Which sounds insanely complex and miserable.

But with copy and paste it was very, very easy to create.

Here is what the first part of that query looks like in SQL:

```
Ebook Sales By Month

SELECT DISTINCTROW Pronoun.Month, Pronoun.Year, [Ebook Link Table].Title, Pronoun.ISBN, Sum(Pronoun.Copies) AS SumOfCopies, Sum(Pronoun.[Payable Earnings]) AS [SumOfPayable Earnings] 'Pronoun' AS Platform
FROM [Ebook Link Table] RIGHT JOIN Pronoun ON [Ebook Link Table].[Pronoun ISBN] = Pronoun.ISBN
GROUP BY Pronoun.Month, Pronoun.Year, [Ebook Link Table].Title, Pronoun.ISBN
HAVING (((Sum(Pronoun.[Payable Earnings]))>0))

UNION

SELECT DISTINCTROW [Other Ebook].MonthOfSale, [Other Ebook].YrOfSale, [Ebook Link Table].Title, [Other Ebook].ASIN, Sum([Other Ebook].Quantity) AS SumOfQuantity, Sum([Other Ebook].Profit) AS SumOfProfit, 'StoryBundle' AS Platform
FROM [Other Ebook] LEFT JOIN [Ebook Link Table] ON [Other Ebook].ASIN = [Ebook Link Table].ASIN
GROUP BY [Other Ebook].MonthOfSale, [Other Ebook].YrOfSale, [Ebook Link Table].Title, [Other Ebook].ASIN

UNION

SELECT DISTINCTROW Nook.Month, Nook.Year, [Ebook Link Table].Title, Nook.[BN ID / ISBN], Sum(Nook.[Net Units Sold]) AS [SumOfNet Units Sold], Sum(Nook.[Total Royalty]) AS [SumOfTotal Royalty], 'Nook' AS Platform
FROM [Ebook Link Table] RIGHT JOIN Nook ON [Ebook Link Table].Nook = Nook.[BN ID / ISBN]
WHERE (((Nook.[List Price])>0))
GROUP BY Nook.Month, Nook.Year, [Ebook Link Table].Title, Nook.[BN ID / ISBN]
HAVING (((Nook.[BN ID / ISBN]) Not Like "978*"))

UNION
```

This portion is combining data from three different queries, one each for Pronoun, Other Ebook, and Nook.

And actually, because it's a copy of the SQL language in those queries, it's pulling directly from the source tables.

Looks insane, right? But if you set it up correctly it's not hard to create at all.

For this particular query, for each of my twelve revenue sources, I wanted a query that gave me Month, Year, Title, Identifier, Units, and Revenue. That's easy enough to build. You know how to do that at this point. It's a summary query built off of a single table.

So you set that up, one query for each source. And then you go to the Create tab and in the Queries section you click on Query Design instead of Query Wizard.

This opens a new query in Design View that has no tables or queries selected. It's a blank slate.

You'll see a Show Table dialogue box. Close that because we're not going to work in Design View.

Now, switch over your view to SQL View.

(You can either do that by clicking on SQL View under the Results section of the Query Tools Design tab, by right-clicking into the work area and choosing SQL View from the dropdown menu, or by going to the Home tab and changing your view from there.)

You should see the word SELECT visible in your workspace with a semi-colon after it. Delete that.

Now open your first source query and go to SQL View for that query. The entirety of the SQL language for that query will already be highlighted. Copy it. (Ctrl + C)

Go back to your new query workspace and paste what you copied. (Ctrl + V)

Delete the semi-colon from the end of what you just pasted.

Hit Enter twice. (You really don't have to do this but I find it's visually cleaner if I do.)

Type UNION and hit enter two more times.

Open your second source query and copy that over to your new query the same way you did with the first source query.

If you have a third query to add then delete the semi-colon, hit Enter a couple times, type UNION, hit enter a couple more times, and copy the next source into your query.

Keep going until all of your sources have been added.

As long as you built your queries to have identical columns, to only include the columns/fields you wanted in your union query, and to have the same data types, then you should be done at this point.

The last query you paste in should have your closing semi-colon. None of the others should have one. Each query is connected with UNION.

To see if it worked, change your view to Datasheet View. If it did, you should see the information from your source queries all combined into one table nice and neat.

If it didn't, you'll probably get an error message and will need to check that each query has the same number of columns and that they match up in terms of type of data in each column.

In the example above, if I have to add a new data source I usually forget that that last column 'Pronoun' AS Platform is one that I've added into the union query itself and so I usually end up getting an error message and then having to add that in for my newest data source.

To save yourself that headache, spend the time to get your source queries completely matched up.

Another thing to know is that your union query when you look at the data may have the different sources intermingled. One of my union queries sorts on date, so the results of the various source queries are blended together by date. That's why I have that final column, 'X' as Platform for each source I bring in so that I can see which query isn't doing what it should if my data looks wrong.

Just remember if you do add a fixed field like that to do so within the SELECT clause portion of your SQL statement and not after one of the other clauses.

* * *

A few more things to know about union queries.

They are listed at the bottom of your queries and sorted separately from your select queries. You can identify a union query because it is shown with two interlocking circles on the left-hand side of the name as opposed to the two stacked data tables shown for select queries.

There is no Design View for a union query. You can only open it in Datasheet View or in SQL View.

Also, I've never been able to get a union query to keep a summation if I add it to the bottom of the query by using Totals in the Records section of the Home tab. I can add totals while working in the query and see the values at the bottom, but when I close and reopen the query that summation is gone. But, if you click on Totals again it will come right back.

(On their website Microsoft provides a workaround for how to permanently add a summary line to your union query but it's pretty ugly and I'm not inclined to use it.)

You can include an ORDER BY clause at the end of your SQL statement to set the sort order for your query. I generally just do this in Datasheet View and save when I close rather than try to write it in SQL.

Access will take the field names for your query from the field names used in the first query you pasted in. So if you want to control the field names be sure to paste in the query that has the field names you want first.

If you're pasting in an entire table, you can use

SELECT * from [Table Name]

instead of pasting in the individual selected field names.

Also, as mentioned in *Access 2019 Beginner*, when I changed my field names using the Field Name: Field Name Description format, it broke a couple of my union queries but not all of them.

I believe that the ones where I had copied and pasted the entire SQL text from an existing query updated correctly, but the ones where I'd cleaned up the SQL text or typed it in myself were the ones that broke.

When those broke I knew it had happened because I saw an Enter Parameters dialogue box appear when I tried to open the union query the next time.

Also, I talked in this entire section about using queries to generate your union query but technically you can use tables as well. You just need to know how to create the SQL statement to do that.

Since I think it's easier to create a query first and then just copy and paste that over, I didn't cover it here. But you can see in the screenshot above with the three pasted in queries exactly how you could write something like that. Each of those pasted in portions are in fact pulling data directly from the source tables.

# Queries: Crosstab Queries

Another type of query that I sometimes use is called a crosstab query. I don't use it often, because I normally just dump my query results into Excel and use a PivotTable instead. But the nice thing about crosstab queries as opposed to the dumping into Excel method is that you only have to create them that one time.

What a crosstab query does is it puts one set of values across the top of the table, another across the left-hand side and then at the intersection of those two values it shows you the result for the two variables you're combining.

For example, I have a few names I write under and I like to sometimes look at how many words I've published for each author for each year. Since I track year published and wordcount for every title I publish, this is an easy crosstab query to create.

It has year across the top, author name down the side, and a total wordcount for each combination of year and author at the intersection of the two.

Let's walk through how to do that.

I use the Query Wizard for this which means that I need a single table or query that has all of my information in it. (If you're very comfortable in Access you can create a crosstab query that uses more than one table or query, but we're not going to cover that here, because you can't use the Query Wizard to do that.)

First step. Choose the Query Wizard from the Queries section of the Create tab. (You don't have to click on the table or query you want to use at this point because it will ignore you anyway.)

In the first screen of the Query Wizard choose Crosstab Query Wizard and click OK.

This will bring up the Crosstab Query Wizard dialogue box where you need to choose the table or query you want to use.

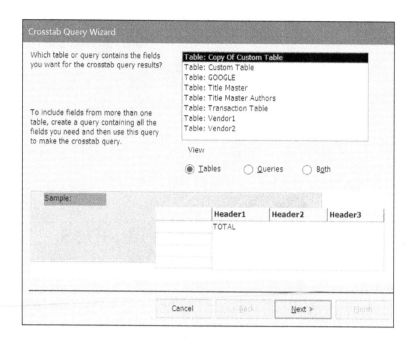

Note that by default it shows your tables, but you can change that by clicking on the circle next to Queries or the circle next to Both right below the table listing.
    Choose the table or query you want to use and then click Next.

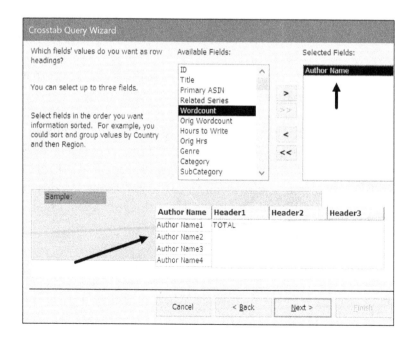

Now it's time to choose your row headings. This is the variable you want along the side of your crosstab query result. (For some reason the way they phrase this question I always think it's my column headers but it's not.) For me this is going to be Author Name.

When you choose a field, it will display that field name in the preview screen at the bottom of the dialogue box, like you can see above.

You can select up to three fields for your row headings, just keep in mind that if the three fields are not exclusively related to one another (like title, author, series generally would be) that this will increase the number of rows in your table because there will be a row for each unique combination of your three selected fields.

After you've chosen your row headings, click Next.

Now you can select the field to use for your column headings. The preview down below will show whichever field you're currently clicked onto as the header field. When I choose Year Pub for that, it shows below Year Pub1, Year Pub2, Year Pub 3 as the sample values.

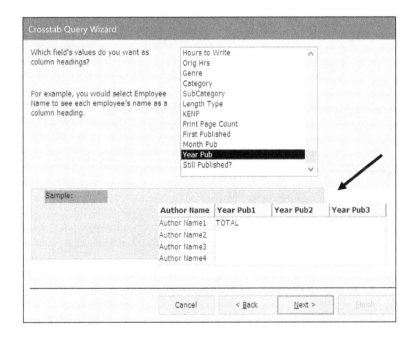

You can only choose one field here. (PivotTables will let you choose more, but this does not.)

After you've chosen your field, click Next.

If you chose a date field your next option will be what time interval to use for your dates, Year, Quarter, Month, Date, or Date/Time.

Once more, the preview does not show actual dates from your data. It just shows generic examples of what those column headers will look like under each option. If you have a date field, make your selection, and click Next.

If you chose a numeric or text field instead of a date field, Access will go straight to the screen which asks what calculation to make in the table.

Click on the field you want to use for your calculation. I'm going to use Wordcount for mine. And then click on the type of calculation you want to perform. I want Sum.

In the preview section you should then see the function and field you've chosen in the white space between the column and row fields you chose, like so:

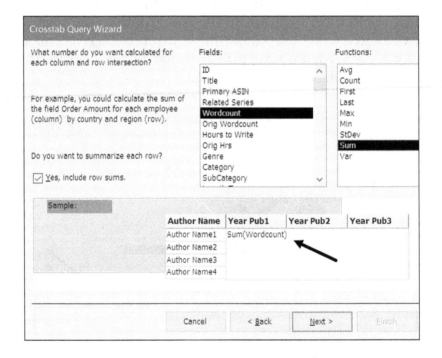

Also, this is where you can tell Access if you want a column added to your table that shows the total value for each row. I tend to leave that checked because I do want to see the total for each row, but if you don't care about that you can uncheck it.

(The reason you might want to uncheck it is because Access puts it in a weird place and when you have additional values added to the table over time it's even weirder. I'll show you in a moment.)

Click Next.

Change your query name if you want. If you don't it will be your source file name with Query_Crosstab added at the end. I tend to name mine by the column, row, and calculation field I'm using. So I'd do Wordcount by Year Per Author.

I always choose to view the query, but if you are comfortable enough in Access that this was just a base for you to work from, then you might choose modify the design to see the query in Design View instead.

Click Finish.

And here you go:

| Author Name ▾ | Total Of Wor ▾ | 2013 ▾ | 2014 ▾ | 2015 ▾ | 2016 ▾ |
|---|---|---|---|---|---|
| Author A | 1260375 | | | 69330 | |
| Author B | 322342 | | | | |
| Author C | 239707 | | 70050 | 169657 | |
| Author C/Autho | 74877 | | 8669 | | 7998 |
| Author D | 269849 | 59990 | 39104 | 14639 | 90281 |
| Author E | 38976 | | 14351 | 24625 | |
| Author F | 574520 | | | 109000 | 93305 |
| Author G | 216807 | 27278 | 53614 | 32441 | 30142 |
| Author H | 211265 | | | 98825 | 106458 |

A few things to note.

The summary column for each row is the *second* column instead of showing at the end of the table. It's easy enough to left-click on the column and drag it to the end, which is what I always do with these queries.

But because Access by default wants to put that summary column on the left-hand side, I find that when new columns of data are added to a crosstab query (such as a new year of data) that the new data is added to the right-hand side of the summary column.

So I have to move the summary column again or it ends up stuck in the middle between the entries that were already in the table and the new ones.

At this point there is also not a summary for each column. I can't see the totals for 2013, 2014, etc.

To add one, use the Totals option in the Records section of the Home tab and then go through for each column and select Sum in the Total row.

Just like with a union query, when you save, close, and later reopen the crosstab query that totals row will not be visible. But if you click once more on Totals in the Records section of the Home tab it will reappear for any column where you added a sum.

One final adjustment I make to my crosstab queries is to rename that totals column which you can do in Design View.

Another thing to note about the totals column. If you realize you chose the wrong field for your calculation, you need to adjust the totals column separate from the summary column.

So, for example, I originally generated this table using a field called Wordcount but I meant to use a field called Orig Wordcount. (It's the difference between how many words are in a book and how many of those words were original to that book. So a collection of three titles might have a wordcount of 100,000 but no original wordcount.)

When I went into Datasheet View and changed the field from Wordcount to Orig Wordcount my summary column did not change. I had to go to that column and change it as well from Wordcount to Orig Wordcount. Like so:

| Field: | Author Name | Year Pub | Orig Wordcount | Total Wordcount: [Orig Wordcount] | |
|---|---|---|---|---|---|
| Table: | Title Master Authors | Title Master Authors | Title Master Authors | Title Master Authors | |
| Total: | Group By | Group By | Sum | Sum | |
| Crosstab: | Row Heading | Column Heading | Value | Row Heading | |
| Sort: | | | | | |
| Criteria: | | | | | |
| or: | | | | | |

Same applies to any formatting change you make. The individual entries and the summary column must be changed separately in the Property Sheet.

\* \* \*

One final note. Your crosstab queries will be listed in their own section above your select queries and will show with an image next to them of a single data table with a darker first row and a darker first column.

# Queries: Ask for User Input in a Query

Another type of query that you may want to use is a parameter query that asks users to provide input values that are then used as calculations in your query.

I've never had to use this one but I can see where it might come in handy if you've written a query that includes a calculation but there is a part of that calculation that can vary.

Say, for example, that I have a query that lists a series of loans I've made where I'm expecting payment. And that I want to discount the value of those loans by a certain percentage based upon how many people I expect to default on their payments. But that that percentage varies over time. When the economy is good, most people pay what they owe. When it's bad, though, a lot more people stop paying.

In that case, I can set up my query so that every time I run it, it asks me to provide the discount rate. It's far better to do that than run the query with a fixed discount rate baked into an equation in the query and have to remember to change it. (Also, that goes against good data principles where you show your assumptions.)

\* \* \*

To create a parameter query that will ask a user for a value, open your query in Design View.

If it's important that the query or your ultimate report contain your assumed value (and I'd argue that's generally the case), then create a new field for that value with whatever name you want to assign it and a description of what it needs in brackets.

For example, if I want to have a field named Royalty Split, then I might write:

Royalty Split: [Enter Royalty Split Percent]

for my new field in Design View.

That would give me a column labeled Royalty Split and every single time I opened that query I would see an Enter Parameter Value dialogue box that said "Enter Royalty Split Percent".

The one thing here that you can't have is Royalty Split: [Royalty Split] because it will create a circular reference and refuse to run. So your field name has to be different from whatever you put in brackets for the dialogue box to display.

Also, don't make your text in the brackets the same as any of your field names or else Access will just treat it like a reference to that field.

If you do it this way, you can then also have a calculation in the query that uses the value provided in that field.

Here I've created the fields Party 1 Payout and Party 2 Payout and used my Royalty Split value to calculate the payout for each party. You'll note that I also changed the Royalty Split text to tell the user to enter the value as a decimal. I could have written the equation differently instead, but chose to do it this way.

When I then change the view to Datasheet View, Access shows the parameter dialogue box asking for my Royalty Split value.

You can see that the text I put in brackets, "Enter Royalty Split Percent as a Decimal" is shown above the input box.

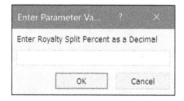

In this case I am going to enter a value of .6 so that the two columns have different results. When I click on OK my data table appears with the three columns. The input column shows the value I provided, .6, and the other two columns show the Royalty amount split 60/40 between the two parties.

| Royalty | Royalty Split | Party 1 Payout | Party 2 Payout |
|---|---|---|---|
| $9.42 | .6 | $5.65 | $3.77 |
| $13.92 | .6 | $8.35 | $5.57 |
| $5.00 | .6 | $3.00 | $2.00 |
| $2.50 | .6 | $1.50 | $1.00 |

\* \* \*

I gave the new input variable its own field because I like to have all assumptions visible so that anyone looking at my data can see what's happening. But you don't have to do that.

You can just create the calculation and have it ask for the value. But if you do it that way be sure to leverage the bracketed portion of your new input so that users know what to provide.

So instead of using something like:

Party 1 Payout: [Royalty Split]*[Royalty]

you'd want to use:

Party 1 Payout: [Enter Royalty Split as a Decimal]*[Royalty]

This would give the same result, but it would make sure that the parameter dialogue box that the user saw said "Enter Royalty Split as a Decimal".

\* \* \*

Alright. There you have it. Basically treat the text you want the user to see in your Enter Parameter Value dialogue box as a named field with brackets around it wherever you want to collect that information. And if you do so in a separate field then you can name that field and use the field name in any other expressions you write.

# Queries: A Brief Mention of Other Query Types

As I've mentioned previously, I use Access as an Excel user who needs more capability than Excel can give me. I do not use it as a computer programmer or database developer. This means that I use it more for analysis than I do as a standalone database. Which means that there are additional query types that I don't use because they're more the types of queries someone would use for maintaining a database than analyzing data.

But I wanted to mention them briefly in case you ever need one so that you know they exist and what to call them. All of the queries below are very powerful and have the ability to significantly transform your database, so use them with caution and definitely backup your database first. You can wipe out data with the click of a button with some of these queries and you won't be able to get it back.

Proceed with caution and be sure it's what you want to do before you act.

## Append Query

Append queries allow you to update a table in your database using other records in that same database. So, as I mentioned before, I used to use Append queries to update a table of total sales by month before I figured out how to use a union query to get that information instead.

I actually currently use two append queries because I ran into an issue where I was trying to track monthly profit and loss by title and I had months where I'd advertised a title but not sold a copy of that title. The way I'd built my profit and loss calculations was missing that ad expense for those titles.

So I now have two append queries that capture all titles for each month where I either had a sale OR had ad spend and put them in a table for me. I then use a query to take all unique month-title combinations from that table and use that as my "anchor" to build my monthly profit and loss by title calculations.

The way to create an append query is to create a basic select query and then transform it into an append query where you map the fields in the query to the table where you want to append your results. So Title to Title, Author to Author, etc.

You run an append query as opposed to opening it to view results in a data table. Nothing happens until you click on the Run exclamation mark in the Results section of the Query Tools Design tab.

## Make-Table Query

I have never used a make-table query, but according to Access this is a query you would use to merge two existing tables of data or to make a new table out of a query. One advantage here is that the new table can be in a different database.

Be careful here, because when you create the new table it is now standalone and no longer connected to its source data. You basically create a select query, convert it to a make-table query, tell Access where to put the new table, and then run it.

## Update Query

You can use an update query to update the value of a specific field in a table. It's a bit like using the Find and Replace function but amped up a lot more. It can only be used on existing records, not to add or delete a record.

Be very careful when using an update query since it is possible to update records in more than one table at a time.

## Find Duplicate Records Query

There is a Query Wizard for this one. You tell it which tables and which fields in those tables you want to compare. This is a good query to use with a multi-user database where more than one person may have entered the same information.

## Delete Records Query

You basically create a query that contains the records you want to delete and then in Design View change the query over to a delete query from a select query and run it.

But be very, very careful here because if you didn't actually use any criteria to narrow down your results then you'll delete all of the content in your table with one little click.

# Forms: An Overview

Okay, then. Now that we're done with queries, on to forms.

The type of form we're going to cover here is what's referred to as a bound form because it ties back to a table or query with data in it that can be viewed and/or amended via the use of the form interface in Access.

As I mentioned in *Access 2019 Beginner* a form can be a user-friendly way to present the information in a table. Rather than force someone to view the information in a grid of columns and rows you can present that same information in a one-page-per-record format that is organized for ease of use.

For all of the forms we're going to discuss below, it won't actually be saved in your database until you choose to save it or choose to close and save it. That will also be when you have the opportunity to name the form.

## Basic Form

For lack of a better term, the "basic" form option provides all the information related to one record on a single page. You create a basic form in Access by clicking on your source table or query, going to the Forms section of the Create tab, and clicking on Form.

You will then see a page in the main workspace that contains all of the fields from the source object with values pulled from the first record in that source. Here, for example, is the first record from the parameter value query we were just looking at. It asked me to provide the royalty split before it opened and then populated the form with that value and those calculations.

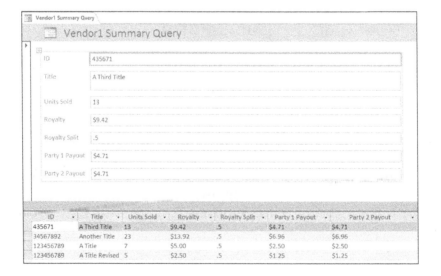

There should also be a property sheet pane on the right-hand side. At the bottom of the workspace you can navigate to each page to see the values for each record using the arrows or changing the number from 1 of X to whatever record you want to see. The 1 there represents the first record not the ID number.

## Split Form

To create a split form, select your table or query, go to the Forms section of the Create tab, and select Split Form from the More Forms dropdown menu.

A split form lets you see both a form version of the data and a datasheet version of the data at the same time. The two views are linked and you can edit the entries in either the form or the datasheet. Using a split form can help you locate a specific record in less time than if you had to search or page through one record at a time.

Clicking into any cell in the datasheet view at the bottom will immediately change the data that is displayed in the form portion up top to match that record. It will also select the corresponding cell for that record in the top portion

The arrows at the bottom of the workspace can still be used to page through the records like in the basic form view. You will also have the property sheet pane visible when the form is first created.

## Multiple Items Form

You can also create a multiple items form which will display more than one record per page.

Even though this option looks a lot like the datasheet view you see with a query or a table, it gives you more control over which fields to include in your form (making it more user-friendly for input or review) and also more control over formatting of your fields.

To create a multiple items form, click on the table or query you want to use, go to the Forms section of the Create tab, click on the dropdown under More Forms, and choose Multiple Items. You'll basically get a grid of rows and columns just like exist in your source query or table.

| ID | Title | Units Sold | Royalty | Royalty Split | Party 1 Payout | Party 2 Payout |
|---|---|---|---|---|---|---|
| 435671 | A Third Title | 13 | $9.42 | .5 | $4.71 | $4.71 |
| 34567892 | Another Title | 23 | $13.92 | .5 | $6.96 | $6.96 |
| 123456789 | A Title | 7 | $5.00 | .5 | $2.50 | $2.50 |
| 123456789 | A Title Revised | 5 | $2.50 | .5 | $1.25 | $1.25 |

Using the arrows at the bottom will move one record at a time.

## Datasheet Form

The datasheet form option looks like your datasheet except it's a form so you have control over formatting. To create it, click on your source table or query, go to the Forms section under the Create tab, and choose Datasheet from the More Forms dropdown menu.

# Reports: An Overview

A report lets you create a nice, summarized printable document that displays your information in a user-friendly way. It can have custom headers, footers, and field labels. You can determine font size and add bolding or italics, change the colors, etc.

It can also have summary statistics at various levels. (I have reports that provide detail information by title but also summarize values at the author and series level as well, for example.)

There are two primary ways to create a report, the Report Tool and the Report Wizard.

## Report Tool

The Report Tool is very simple to use. It will take whatever table or query you're using as the source document and create a report from it that includes all of your fields. To use it, click on the table or query you want to use, go to the Create tab, and click on Report in the Reports section.

You will immediately see a basic report, like this one:

I usually find that I need to refine any report that Access creates for me using the Report Tool, because, as you can see with this one, the fields run off the page to a second page so the report is not immediately printable.

A report generated this way will open in Layout View which is a view where you can edit the report while still seeing what it will look like on the page. (We'll talk about form and report views more in a minute.)

# Report Wizard

Your other option is to use the Report Wizard. This allows you to choose fields from more than one table or query to build your report. (I'll confess here that I'm more comfortable creating a query that combines all of the values I want to use and building a report from there, but that's probably just my own nervousness at play.)

Click on the first table or query you want to use, go to the Create tab, and click on Report Wizard in the Reports section. This will bring up the Report Wizard dialogue box.

Just like with the query wizard, you can then choose the fields you want to use. And just like with the query wizard, if you choose fields from more than one source you need to have relationships established between those tables and queries beforehand.

Click Next when you're done choosing your fields.

You'll then be asked if you want to group your data on any of your selected fields.

Grouping your data, which we'll discuss more later, essentially displays it by the values for that field. So if I group on year, then my data will be listed based on the year with details underneath each year heading.

Here I've chosen to group on title. Note how that field is now shown as a label above the other fields:

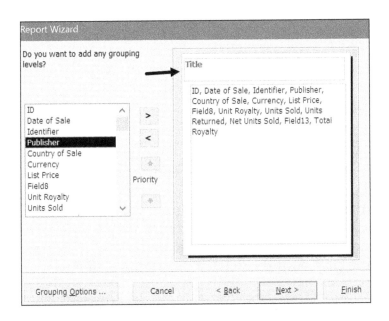

If you click on the Grouping Options button after you've selected at least one field to group by, you can then choose to group text based on X number of letters or your numeric values based on the 10s, 100s, etc. (I don't really use either one but this would let you, for example, have all of your A entries together followed by all of your B entries, etc.)

If you group on more than one field, you can use the Priority arrows to prioritize which field is used first.

When you're done choosing the fields to group by, click Next to go to a screen which will let you choose how to sort your data as well as how to summarize your data.

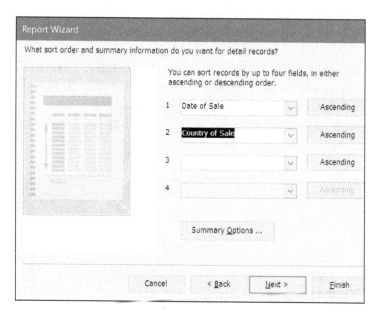

Here I've chosen to sort by Date of Sale and then by Country of Sale, both in ascending order.

Clicking on the Summary Options button allows you to tell Access if you want to take the sum, average, min, or max of any of your numeric values. On the right-hand side, you can choose to do so and only display the summary values or to do so and display both the detail and summary values.

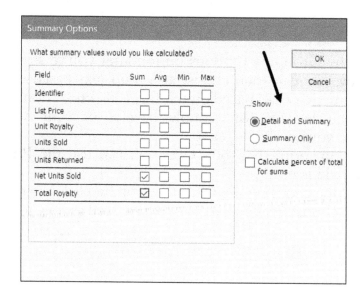

You can also choose to calculate the percent of the total for your summed values on the right-hand side as well. (I generally don't do so.)

Click OK to close Summary Options and Next to move to the next screen where you have the choice between a Stepped, Block, or Outline layout for your report. Clicking on each option will give you a generic preview of that option on the left-hand side of the dialogue box.

You can also choose here to adjust the field width so that all of the fields fit onto the page and choose a Portrait or Landscape orientation. If you have many columns of data, choosing the Landscape orientation will help the data better fit on the page.

When you're done, click Next. Change your report name if you want. Click Finish.

I chose to fit everything on the page in Landscape view, but as you can see here, that didn't work out so well because some of my data doesn't show given the column width and has been replaced with ######### signs. Also, some of my column headers are overlapping one another.

This is why I prefer to build my reports myself starting with the Report Tool, but it is something to work from, so if you're completely at a loss for how to create summary rows or get all of your columns fitting on the page, it does do that.

## Other Options

In addition to Report and Report Wizard you also have Report Design which opens a blank report in Design View and lets you build your report completely from scratch, and Blank Report which does the same thing but in Layout View.

The reports section also lets you create mailing labels, but as I've said before I think there are far better off-the-shelf commercial solutions for customer contact databases these days so I'll just mention that capability but I'm not going to cover it.

# Forms and Reports: Views

We're about to talk about how to work with an existing form or report to customize it and since it's pretty much the same for both of them I'm going to cover a lot of this material together. But first I want to walk through the view options you have available to you.

As a reminder, you can always change your view in the Home tab using the View dropdown. However, with Forms and Reports, you can also right-click in the unused space in a form or report and choose your view from the dropdown menu that way. Also, in Layout View and Design View there is a View dropdown in the Design tab.

## Form View

This is the default view when you open an existing form and is what your finished product looks like. It has all of your data showing.

You can navigate to each record using the arrows at the bottom or by inputting the record number you want. If the data on a specific page is more than you can see in the workspace there will also be scroll bars you can use.

In Form View, you can change values if the form was based upon a table or a basic query with fields that tied directly back to a table. You can't change summary values.

You can move between cells in a form using the arrow keys or Tab and Shift + Tab.

# Report View

This is the default view when you open an existing report. It too shows all of your final data.

In the Report View it's all one large page even if it will print on multiple pages. You can use the scroll bars on the right-hand side to scroll upward and downward, or on the bottom of the workspace to scroll to the left or the right.

Values in a report cannot be edited, but you can click into a cell and use the Tab and Shift + Tab keys to move between values. (Although I've never seen a need to do so.)

# Print Preview

Print Preview is available as a view option for reports, but not for forms. If you select this view it will show you the report one printable page at a time. This is the view that lets you see if any of your columns run onto a second page or if any of your groups break in a way that you don't like.

You can navigate between the printable pages using the arrows or input box at the bottom of the workspace. Use the scroll bars to see the parts of the page that aren't currently visible in the workspace.

You may not actually be able to see the entire page by default because of the zoom level of your workspace. To change the zoom level, you can use the slider in the bottom right corner of the screen. Just click and drag the white bar to the left until the full page is visible in your workspace. Keep in mind that doing so may make the document too small for you to read the text, but it does give a good idea of the visual presentation of your data.

To return to Report View, click on Close Print Preview under the Close Preview section of the Print Preview tab.

I should also note here that while forms don't have a view option of Print Preview you can still choose to Print from the File tab and then choose Print Preview there if you want to see how a form will print.

# Layout View

The Form View, Report View, and Print Preview all just let you look at the form or report in question, but they don't let you edit it. That can only be done in the Layout View and the Design View.

Layout View keeps the form or report looking mostly the same as it will when it prints, except now you have the ability to make edits to your form or report.

You can right-click on a column and see all sorts of available options or you can use the Layout Tools tabs up top to change the design, arrangement, format, or, for reports, page setup.

Here is a report in layout view:

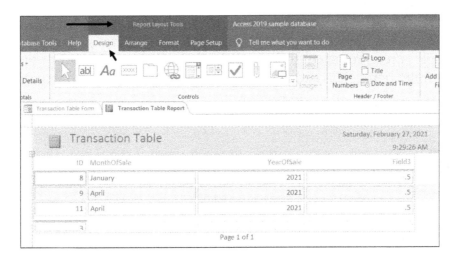

You can see up top that there is a Report Layout Tools header with four tabs under it, Design, Arrange, Format, and Page Setup.

If you right-click on a field name, you will also see a very large dropdown menu with a number of choices available.

# Design View

Design View is very similar to Layout View when you only have a few rows of data. It works with the underlying template instead of showing your results. Here is that same report from above in Design View.

Design View also has a Design Tools header with Design, Arrange, and Format tabs as well as for reports, Page Setup.

There are also options listed when you right-click a field. And there is a Property Sheet for each field that lets you see how it's currently formatted and amend that formatting.

I suspect most people would prefer to work in Layout View. I personally prefer Design View. When a report is long and complicated, I can see everything on one single screen most of the time.

For example, here is a screenshot of Design View for a nine-page report.

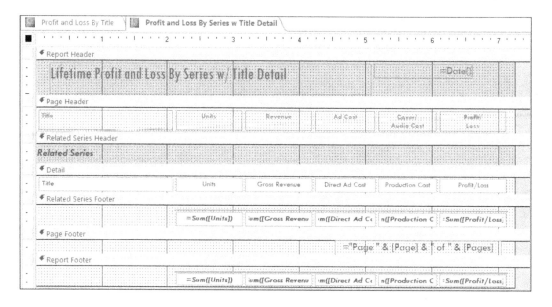

In Layout View I'd have to work with this report across all of those pages, but in Design View it's compacted down to just this small space.

The problem with working in Design View though is that it's harder to tell when an entry doesn't fit or columns go off the edge of the page. So when I do work in Design View I have to frequently switch to Form or Report View to make sure that what I've done works in that view as well.

There are always trade-offs.

# Forms and Reports: Edit and Format Text Boxes

As discussed above, if you want to edit a form or report you need to do so either in Layout View or Design View. There are usually at least two ways to change formatting, one involving the Property Sheet and one involving the Design, Arrange, and Format tabs at the top of the screen.

If you open a form or report in Layout or Design View you will notice that the Design, Arrange, and Format tabs I mentioned above are actually shown under a header section. Depending on which you opened and which view you chose that could be Form Layout Tools, Report Layout Tools, Form Design Tools, or Report Design Tools.

Normally in telling you where to go to perform a task I would reference those header sections, but I'm not going to here because regardless of which one you're in the steps I'm going to discuss remain the same and the tab names remain the same.

So I'll just be referring to the Design, Arrange, and Format tabs which are the tabs displayed under those headers.

I tend to use the Property Sheet because it's all right there in one spot, but the tabs are probably the more user-friendly option.

When you switch to either Layout or Design View the Property Sheet should be visible on the right-hand side of the screen. Here's what a portion of it looks like for a Title field in a report:

The scroll bars on the right-hand side allow you to see the remainder of the options that can be set via the property sheet.

If the property sheet isn't visible, you can go to the Design tab and click on Property Sheet in the Tools section. Or you can right-click on the workspace for the form or report and choose Properties from the dropdown menu.

Another note before we begin, Ctrl + Z to Undo does seem to work when formatting forms or reports and does work for more than one formatting change at a time, so if you mess up simply Ctrl + Z to Undo until you're back to what you had before and then try again.

Also, Access distinguishes between labels and text boxes. Labels contain fixed values and are usually associated with a text box that displays the actual data for a record.

Think of labels as your column headers in a data table or query and text boxes as your values for each record from that table or query. They look a lot alike and can generally be edited in the same way, so from here on out I'm going to refer to them generically as text boxes unless what I say only applies to one or the other.

And, finally, for all of the options below you need to click on the text box you want to edit before you make your edit. I'll explicitly state that for the first few so you get the hang of it, but then I'm just going to assume that you know to do so.

## Resize a Text Box

To change the size of a text box you have a few options.

You can click on the box you want to change and then move your cursor until it's along the edge of the box and you see a two-sided arrow either pointing to the left and right (for the side edges) or up and down (for the top and bottom edges). You can then left-click and drag the box to the desired size at that point.

Usually this will change the width of all associated text boxes. Depending on the nature of the box that you're formatting it may be all boxes in that column or it may be all boxes in that row. And sometimes it depends on whether you're changing the height or the width.

So, for example, I just changed the height of an ID label box and it also changed the height of the ID text box in the same row of that form. But when I change the width of that same ID label box it changed the width of all of the other label boxes that were in the same column.

If all the text boxes don't change at once and you wanted them to, you can select multiple text boxes by using the Ctrl key as you click on each one, and then when you click and drag on one text box it will resize them all.

Your other option for resizing a text box is to click into the box you want to change and in the Property Sheet on the right-hand side of the screen change the values for Width and/or Height. (About the fourth or fifth listed choices.)

This too will most likely change the width and height for the entire column or row, depending on the nature of the change and the relationship between the boxes. For example, if I change the width of a header row label box it won't necessarily change the width of the detailed content text box below. But if I change the text box it will change all related text boxes in that column.

## Remove the Border Around a Text Box

If you don't want a visible border around a text box in your form or report, you can:

Select the box or boxes you want to modify, go to the Control Formatting section of the Format tab, click on the Shape Outline dropdown arrow, and choose Transparent.

You can also click on the dropdown arrow under Shape Outline, go to the Line Type option at the bottom, and chose the blank line choice which is at the very top of the Line Type dropdown.

Note that this will work with Design View as well as Layout View but that you won't be able to see that the format change is in effect in the workspace in

Design View. The box will still look like it has borders around it. However, your change will be reflected in the Property Sheet and you will be able to see it if you switch to Form or Report View.

Your other option to remove the visible border from around a box is to use the Property Sheet. The option you want to change there is called Border Style and is about eleven rows down. Once more, you want the Transparent option which you can find in the dropdown menu available when you click into the field.

## Add a Border Around a Text Box

To add a border around a box, you have the same options you had for removing the border.

You can use the Shape Outline dropdown in the Format tab to choose your line type. (For a simple border it's the single line which is the second option in the Line Type dropdown.)

Or you can use the Property Sheet to change the Border Style.

Both give you an option of solid, dashes, short dashes, dots, sparse dots, dash dot, and dash dash dot for your line style.

## Change the Color or Thickness of the Border Around a Text Box

If you want to change the color of the line around a text box, go to the Shape Outline dropdown in the Format tab, and choose a different color.

Or you can change the selection in the Border Color dropdown in the Property Sheet which is just below the Border Style option.

With the property sheet, to see the same color options that you have in the Format tab, click on the ... next to the dropdown arrow for Border Color.

That will bring up a listing of 130 colors to choose from arranged in Theme Colors and Standard Colors. There is also the More Colors option to choose a custom color.

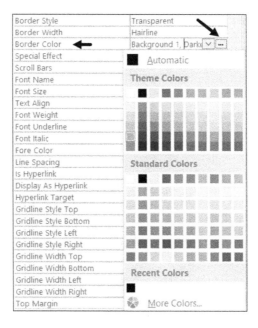

If you want to change the width of the line used for the border, this can be done in the Shape Outline dropdown by choosing a different option for Line Thickness. In the Property Sheet the change can be made under Border Width.

In the Shape Outline dropdown the lines are shown visually at different widths. In the property sheet you have to choose a pt width for your line. The higher the pt value the thicker the line.

## Add Grid Lines Around Text Boxes

In addition to the basic line you can add around a text box, you can also add what Access calls a gridline. These are separate from your Border Style.

In the image below there are four text boxes with a simple black border. They also all four have a grid line along the top. It is separate from the text box, but associated with it.

I always add gridlines using the Property Sheet, so we'll cover that option first, but you can also do so through the Arrange tab.

In the Property Sheet there are four rows that let you add gridlines called Gridline Style Top, Gridline Style Bottom, Gridline Style Left, and Gridline Style Right. And then below that are rows for Gridline Color and for determining the width of each of the four types of gridline.

| | |
|---|---|
| Gridline Style Top | Solid |
| Gridline Style Bottom | Transparent |
| Gridline Style Left | Transparent |
| Gridline Style Right | Transparent |
| Gridline Color | Background 1, Darker 35% |
| Gridline Width Top | 2 pt |
| Gridline Width Bottom | 1 pt |
| Gridline Width Left | 1 pt |
| Gridline Width Right | 1 pt |

(You can find these options towards the bottom of the visible property sheet choices about 26 rows down.)

The gridline style choices are the same as for a border: Transparent, Solid, Dashes, Short Dashes, etc. But the line you add can be a single line on the top, bottom, or either side of a text box. For this reason, gridlines are a good choice for separating out summary values, like in the example above. You put a thick grid line above the text box that contains the summary value to distinguish it from the values it's summing up.

You can change the color of the gridline using the Gridline Color box and you can make the line thicker using the Gridline Width box for each gridline. The example above used a 2 pt gridline with a color of Background 1, Darker 35%.

Often when you're adding sums into a report Access will include gridlines for you by default. To remove an existing gridline change the Gridline Style to Transparent.

Your other option for gridlines is to go to the Table section of the Arrange tab where it says Gridlines. Click on the dropdown arrow under Gridlines to see your available choices.

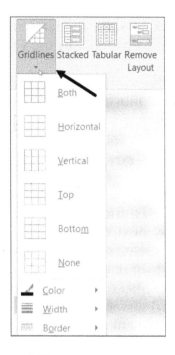

Choosing Both will put four gridlines around your text box. Horizontal will put a top and bottom gridline. Vertical will put a left and right gridline. Top will put one on top of the text box. Bottom will put one on the bottom of the text box. None will remove any existing gridlines.

When you make a new choice, it overrides your old choice, so if you want a strange gridline combination like one side and the bottom you'd have to do that in the Property Sheet.

You can also change the color, line width, and line style using the Color, Width, and Border options in the dropdown. These changes can be made either before you insert your gridline or after you insert it.

## Change the Background Color of a Text Box

To fill a label or text box with a color, you can go to the Format tab, choose Shape Fill, and select your color from there.

Or you can change the Back Color option in the Property Sheet. (About the eighth option listed.) If you use the Property sheet click on the … to see all available colors. A color you've already set via the Format tab may be listed as Accent 1 and you'll need to click on the … to see what the actual color used was.

When you change the background color of a text box it will be immediately visible in both Layout View and Design View.

If you need to revert back to the original settings, the default background color for the base theme is Background 1 in the Property Sheet or Automatic in the Shape Fill dropdown.

(Just now I didn't have Background 1 as an option in my property sheet, but it let me type it in. When in doubt I usually check a field nearby that has the formatting I want and then change my values to whatever that field is using.)

## Change the Font Color in a Text Box

To change the color of the text in a label or text box, you can either go to the Text Formatting section of the Home tab or the Font section of the Format tab. Click on the dropdown arrow next to the A and choose your font color from there. Or use More Colors to create a custom color.

(Automatic will return the font color to the default color.)

Or you can use the Property Sheet and change the value for Fore Color (which is located a little more than halfway down the list). Use the ... next to the dropdown to see all the available colors.

(To get back to the default color choose Text Black for the standard Access theme or if you're using a different theme then you can copy the description from another field into the one you need to change back. For example, mine was using Text 1, Lighter 50% which wasn't available in the dropdown so I had to copy and paste it in to get back to a text color that matched my other column headings.)

## Change the Font in a Text Box

These instructions are for changing the font in a specific text box. See the next chapter for changing the fonts used in all forms and reports at once.

To change the font used for a particular label or text box, click into the text box, go to the Font section of the Format tab or the Text Formatting section of the Home tab, and select a different font from the dropdown menu.

Or you can go to the Font Name row in the Property Sheet (a little less than halfway down) and choose a new font from the dropdown there.

To change all of the label and text boxes in that one form or report to a different font, use Ctrl + A to select all text boxes first and then make your change. You'll need to use the Format or Home tabs to make that change, not the property sheet.

If you do select more than one label or text box at a time, the dropdown menu for Font may look blank before you make your choice, but that's okay. That's just because the selected text boxes are using more than one font and so it shows as blank since it can't show multiple fonts at once. When you select your new font that will apply to all selected text boxes regardless of the font they were using previously.

## Change the Font Size in a Text Box

My version of Access defaults to an 11 pt font size, but I've found that using an 8 pt font size makes it easier for me to fit all of my data onto one report page so I do this one often.

To change font size you can go to the Font section of the Format tab or the Text Formatting section of the Home tab and select a new font size from the dropdown menu on the right of the font menu. You can also type in the font size you want instead of using the dropdown.

Or you can go to the Font Size option on the Property Sheet (about midway down the list) and change the value there.

Once more, if you select all text boxes in your form or report your best bet is to use the Format tab or Home tab, and selecting more than one text box may mean the dropdown menu is blank until you make your selection.

## Unselect Text Boxes

This is a good point to tell you how to unselect text boxes you've selected because Esc doesn't work in Access the way it does in some of the other programs. The easiest way I've found to unselect text boxes I don't want selected is to just click into a blank space somewhere in the form or report workspace. That will unselect all selected text and label boxes.

## Change the Text in a Label Text Box

If you need to change the text in a label text box, you have a couple of options.

You can double-click on the label box until you see your cursor within that box and then you can replace the text by typing in your new text and deleting the old text.

Or you can change the entry for Caption in the Property Sheet.

This is for label text boxes only. DO NOT change the text of any data text box. Because if you do so Access won't know what field to pull the information from and when you look at your form or report in Form or Report View you'll see #Name? in that field instead of your values. You may also suddenly have an Enter Parameter dialogue box popping up when you try to switch to Form or Report View.

It's absolutely fine to change the text in the label box for those fields, but don't change the data input text that you see in Design or Layout View.

If you think you might do so by accident, then I would suggest you only make changes to field labels in the Property Sheet because for data boxes there is no Caption field that you can change. (The field name the data is pulling from is listed under Control Source for those fields.)

## Add Formatting to a Numeric Data Field

To apply a format to a data field in your form or report, you again have a couple of options.

In the Property Sheet for a data field one of the first options is Format. For data fields with numbers in them there is a dropdown menu where you can choose between General Number, Currency, Euro, Fixed, Standard, Percent, and Scientific with samples that show how each one will look.

(For text you won't have options to choose. The dropdown is blank.)

I tend to use Currency for monetary values which formats my numbers, because I'm in the U.S., using a $ sign and two decimal places. And I use Standard for basic numbers like units sold because it includes a comma separator for any thousands.

To give you an idea of the difference, General would show 1234.56, Currency would show $1,234.56, and Standard would show 1,234.56.

Directly below the Format option is a Decimal places option which I will often set to zero to keep my column widths shorter.

Your other formatting option is the Number section of the Format tab where there is a dropdown menu that gives the same options, General Number, Currency, Euro, Fixed, Standard, Percent, and Scientific.

You can also use the Increase Decimals and Decrease Decimals options below that on the right side to change the number of decimal places that are visible. And the $ sign, % sign, and comma that are below the dropdown are just shortcut ways to change the format of a field to Currency, Percent, and Standard, respectively.

The Number section will be grayed out if a field you are clicked into is not formatted as a number field.

## Change Formatting for a Date Field

By default, Access adds a date field to the top of any report and the date format it uses is Long Date which includes day of the week and a spelled out version of the date. Access also has a field right below that with the Long Time which shows hour, minute, and seconds. I usually delete the time field because it's not important for my reports to have that level of detail. And I like to change the format of the date field.

To change the date format, click on the field, go to the Number section of the Format tab, and in the dropdown that says Long Date, choose a different option from General Date, Medium Date, or Short Date.

You can also go to the Property Sheet and choose your option from the dropdown for the Format field.

I tend to prefer General Date or Short Date for my own reports, but if I were working with an international team I'd probably choose Medium Date since it solves any potential question of whether 3/2/2020 is March 2nd or February 3rd since that can vary depending on what country you're in.

## Bold Text in a Text Box

If you want the text within a text box to be bolded, you can click on the box you want to edit and use Ctrl + B.

Or you can click on the box, go to the Font section of the Format tab or the Text Formatting section of the Home tab, and click on the capital B for bold there.

Or, for the largest number of options, go to the Property Sheet and change the value for Font Weight. There you have the choice of Thin, Extra Light, Light, Normal, Medium, Semi-Bold, Bold, Extra Bold, and Heavy.

To undo bolding of your text, use Ctrl + B, click on the B option in one of the tabs, or change the value in the Property Sheet to Normal. (If you chose a bolding option in the Property Sheet and try to use Ctrl + B to remove it, you may have to use Ctrl + B twice for it to work.)

## Italicize Text in a Text Box

If you want to italicize the text in a text box, select that box, and use Ctrl + I.

You can also click on the slanted I in the Font section of the Format tab or the Text Formatting section of the Home tab.

Or you can change the setting for Font Italic in the Property Sheet to Yes.

To remove italics, use Ctrl + I, click on the slanted I in one of the tabs, or change the Font Italic setting to No in the Property Sheet.

## Underline Text in a Text Box

Note that this is different from adding a solid line under a text box, which would be a gridline.

To underline the text in a text box, you can use Ctrl + U.

You can also click on the underlined U in the Font section of the Format tab or the Text Formatting section of the Home tab.

Or you can change the Font Underline setting to Yes in the Property Sheet.

(Note that you only have the single line underline option available in Access.)

To remove underlining from text, use Ctrl + U, click on the underline U in the tabs, or change the Font Underline setting to No in the Property Sheet.

## Change Text Alignment in a Text Box

By default your text boxes are going to be left-aligned or right-aligned depending on the data type of the field, meaning the values line up with the left-hand side or the right-hand side of their text box.

To change this, click on the field you want to change, and go to the Font section of the Format tab or the Text Formatting section of the Home tab. From there click on the alignment option you want.

The alignment options should be directly under the dropdown for font size. You have left-aligned on the left, centered in the middle, and right-aligned on the right. Each option is a visual representation of how that type of alignment will look.

You can also go to the Property Sheet and change the Text Align option a little more than halfway down the first section. Your options there are General, Left, Center, Right, and Distribute. I'd recommend against using Distribute unless you have a good reason for doing so.

I was also able to use a Ctrl shortcut to center my text (Ctrl + E), but I wouldn't recommend it because it looks like Access also uses that same Ctrl shortcut for a different capability in the online version. A quick glance didn't show this usage of that Ctrl shortcut as an official one for Access.

## "Wrap Text"

In Excel if you wanted all of the text information in a cell visible you'd wrap text so that it carried over onto the next line within that cell instead of being hidden after the text reached the edge of the cell. Access doesn't really have that option.

For text boxes that display your detail results, there is a Can Grow option at the very bottom of the Property Sheet that is generally set to Yes by default. It

220

will change the height of the text box in order to display the full text of your result. For summary values, I recommend just manually changing the height of the text box instead, though.

For your column headers this doesn't exist as an option, so you have to manually adjust the text box height when building your table. You can force part of your text in a label text box onto a new row by using Shift + Enter instead of just Enter at the spot where you want the line break.

## Delete a Text Box

If you want to delete a text box that's currently in your form or report, you can click on that text box, right-click, and choose Delete from the dropdown menu. For Forms this will delete both the label and the data text box.

For Reports it will just delete the text box you clicked on. This means that sometimes the Delete Row or Delete Column option will be the better choice, but just be sure that you're only deleting what you want to delete if you use one of those options.

You can also click onto a text box and use the Delete option from your keyboard. Or you can use the Delete option in the Records section of the Home tab.

## Add a Text Box From Your Source Data

To add a text box to your form or report that is from the source you're using to build the form or report, go to the Design tab and click on Add Existing Fields. This will show you a pane on the right-hand side with the name of all fields available from that source. You can then left-click on the field name you want and drag it into your form or report in the location you want to add it.

Fields come into a form or report in a stacked layout, meaning with the label on the left-hand side and then the value on the right. You can change this under the Arrange tab by choosing Tabular from the Table section. That will change the field display so that the label is in a header row and the values are listed below it.

If you add a new text box and change it to Tabular, it will not be tied to the other text boxes in that row and so will not automatically move with them or resize with them.

(Which is why it's best in my opinion to build a query first that has everything you want in your report and then use that to create the report. Of course, sometimes you don't realize what you want until later and then it's easier to just add one new field instead of reformat an entire report. Although…Hm.

Sometimes reformatting the whole report is easier for me than getting that one silly field to do what I want it to do.)

## Change the Positioning of a Text Box

You can move your text boxes around within your form or report. Often I need to do this after I've added a new text box or deleted ones I didn't want.

In Layout View you can left-click onto the boxes you want to move and drag them to the new location. Just be aware that the label box and the text box with your data in it may move separately, so if that happens you will need to select both of them (using Ctrl) before you drag if you want to keep them together.

In Design View you can also click and drag, but I'll warn you now it's a little finicky and may take a try or two to get your fields where you want them.

Sometimes in Design View you can click and drag on a text box and it won't move at all. In that case you may need to click on the box in the top right corner that shows four arrows in order to move that text box and any other associated text boxes.

Clicking onto that box with the four-sided arrow in it will make sure that your text box moves, but it may also move other text boxes with it. When your data is in columns, this is generally good because it moves the label box as well as any summary box that's associated with your data. But when I was playing with this I found in one instance where it would move three data text boxes and their labels together as a group when I only wanted to move the one.

In that case, which was in a form, in order to reorder those text boxes, I had to click on the data text box for the field that interested me and move it. The label text box automatically moved as well. But I couldn't use the four-sided arrow box at the corner of the label box.

So, basically, you can just click into the data text box you want to move, try it, see what happens and then adjust from there by going back and selecting the label box as well if the label didn't move or by using the four-sided arrow box in the top left corner if the text box won't move at all.

Another way I've found to reposition some text boxes that don't want to move for me is to change the size of the text box instead. So if there's room I'll stretch the text box to where I want it to be on the left or right edge, whichever direction I'm trying to move, and then I'll bring the other side over or change the Width setting on the Property Sheet to what I want it to be.

(As you can see, sometimes my answer to things that don't work in Access is to just poke at them until I make them work somehow someway. Don't be afraid when working on formatting like this to make some mistakes. Like I said, undo seems to actually work well with respect to formatting forms or reports and if you really mess it up, you can always delete and try again. And if you really don't want to lose what you have, right click on your form or report and copy it and then paste in a copy and work on the copy.)

# Forms and Reports: Edit and Format at the Document Level

We just talked about a number of edits you can make at the level of the text entries in your form or report, but there is other formatting that we need to discuss as well. That's the type of formatting that can happen to the overall form or report.

## Change the Size of a Document So It Fits One Page

Often times I find that when I have Access create a report for me and then change the font size and the text box size that it will still carry over to another page even though there's no content left to carry over to that page.

I always fix this in Design View. What you can do there is put your cursor along the right-hand edge of the design space until it turns into a double-sided arrow, and then left-click and drag to the left until the document only takes up one page.

This is only possible if there aren't any text boxes in that space. Usually, that means you're going to first need to move the Page Numbering text box over to the left. You may also need to move the header, but usually it's just the page numbering that still hangs over into the blank area.

## Change the Height of a Section in a Report

If you resize a text box in a section in your report to be taller Access will also resize the space that entire section takes up on the page so that it fits. But if you shrink the height of a text box, Access won't automatically adjust the size of that section of the report. This can lead to there being unsightly space within your report. Like so:

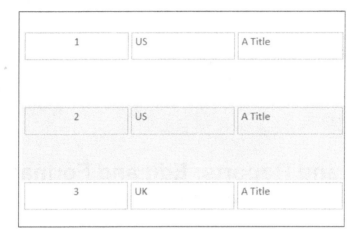

If I look in Design View I can see all that blank space that exists in the Detail section.

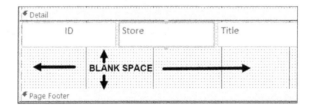

The way to fix this is to go into Design View and hold your cursor along the bottom edge for the section until you see the double-sided arrow pointing upward and downward, and to then left-click and drag until the section below is right under your text box and there's no longer any blank space.

## Page Numbering in Reports

If you use one of the methods we discussed to create your report then by default the report will have page numbering in the bottom right corner of the page.

To move your page number elsewhere in the document, treat it like you would any text box and click and drag.

If you want to use different formatting, you can instead delete the page numbering that's already in your report and replace it.

To add a new page number, go to the Header/Footer section of the Design tab, and click on Page Numbers.

This will bring up the Page Numbers dialogue box where you can choose to have the page numbers display as either Page N of M or just Page N, and where you can set the position for the page numbering as either top of page or bottom of page. You can also set whether the page number shows in the left corner, center, right corner, inside, or outside.

When you use the Page Numbers dialogue box it inserts a new page number, so if you don't delete the old one you'll have two sets of page numbers in your report.

Also, in my opinion, where it by default inserts page numbering on the top of the page is weird since it's below the header section which makes the first page look odd.

Use Ctrl + X and then Ctrl + V if you need to move it from one section of the report to another and it won't let you drag it. When you do so it will likely paste in on the far left-hand side of the section and then you can left-click and drag to where you want it within the section.

If working in Design View, be careful when adding in page numbers that you've added them into the right section of the document. Adding one to Report Footer or Report Header will only include it on the last page of the report or the first page of the report. You want to add to the Page Footer or Page Header section instead.

## Change the Highlighted Rows in Reports

By default, Access will highlight every other row of your results in a report a light gray color. This can make it easier to distinguish values in different rows as you're reading across your document.

However, this highlighting also carries over to any group headings and summary rows you insert in your report. So, for example, in a report grouped by Author, the first author name would be a white row, the next author name would be a gray row, etc. This does not really help with reading comprehension and can look weird, so I prefer to remove it.

To remove highlighting from any section of your report, in Design View select the section header (for example, Detail), and then go to the Format tab, and change the Alternate Row Color dropdown to No Color.

If you want to keep the alternate row colors, but change the color used, you can instead choose a color from that dropdown.

To return to the default color used by Access choose Automatic.

You can also make this change in the Property Sheet. To do so you also need to click on the section header in Design View.

You'll know you've made the correct selection when the Property Sheet options include a row for Back Color and one for Alternate Back Color. Change the value for Alternate Back Color to No Color to remove the lines, Automatic to use the default, or any other color (by using the …) that you want.

And if you want to go really wild (but please don't do it with your Detail section) you can set colors for both Back Color and Alternate Back Color in the Property Sheet. This will color all of your rows for that section, alternating between the Back Color and Alternate Back Color you choose.

If you do so, you will probably also have to change the Back Color for the text boxes in that section as well or they'll remain white while the rest of the row is colored which does not look good.

## Using Themes in Forms and Reports

A quick and easy way to generate a form or report that isn't the Access default is to use themes. These are available in the Themes section of the Design tab when you're in Design or Layout View.

I have ten of them that show as options when I click on the dropdown arrow under Themes. They all come with different colors for the header section of the form or report and some also change the font.

The problem with using a theme is that it will change all of your forms and reports, not just the one you're working on, which can be a little unexpected and disconcerting and may impact how your forms or reports display. If you're going to use a theme do it from the beginning because changes to your font can wreck a previously-formatted form or report since different fonts take up different amounts of space.

## Use Colors in Forms and Reports

Another option for mixing things up is to use the Colors dropdown in the Themes section of the Design tab, which will apply a different color palette to your forms and reports.

Once again, this will happen to all of your forms and reports, not just the one you're working with. Personally, I think the choices look much more exciting in the dropdown than they do on the form or report they're applied to.

# Assigning a New Font Family to Forms and Reports

The final option in the Themes section of the Design tab is the Fonts dropdown. This allows you to assign a different font family for use in all of your forms or reports. If you look at the dropdown you'll see that the first font listed is for the headers in the document and the second one listed is for the data entries.

For example, here I'm using Arial and Times New Roman:

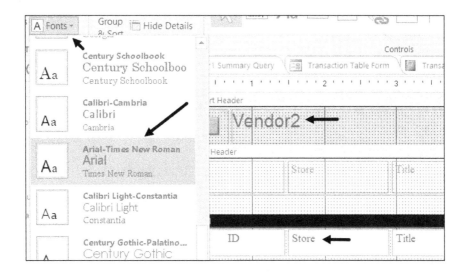

You can see in the background that Vendor2 is in Arial (a sans-serif font, meaning it has no little feet at the bottom of the letters) and the field labels and values, like Store, are in Times New Roman (a serif font that does have little feet at the base of the letters, which you can see if you look at the I in ID or the T in Title.)

# Replace the Logo in a Form or Report

By default the forms and reports generated by Access include a small image in the top left corner. You can go to the Header/Footer section of the Design tab and click on Logo to select an image from your computer to use in its place.

Be careful, because doing so will delete the image that was already there, so that even if you undo you will not get the other image back. (Not that it's so exciting you want it back…)

If the logo you insert doesn't look right, try going to the Property Sheet and while clicked on the logo changing the Size Mode to Stretch or Zoom instead of Clip. (It's about the 6th row down.) For my square logo, for example, Zoom was the best option.

## Controls

The Controls section of the Design tab is really for if you're building a form or report from scratch, which we're not doing here so I'm not going to walk through all of those in detail. At this level of knowledge probably the only one you might want to use is the Label option to insert text that isn't tied to a field of data.

This could be useful for something like a Copyright notice or disclaimer. You just click on the option and then go to your workspace and click and drag up and over until it creates a text box. You can then type into the text box whatever text you wanted to include.

## Stacked vs. Tabular Layout

I touched on this briefly before but there are two main types of layout for your data fields, stacked and tabular. The choice of which to use is available in the Table section of the Arrange tab.

By default forms will be in a stacked format which Access describes as a "layout similar to a paper form, with labels to the left of each field." Reports by default tend to be in a tabular format which Access describes as "a layout similar to a spreadsheet, with labels across the top and data in columns below the labels."

You can change an entire form or report to the opposite format by using Ctrl + A to select all of your text boxes, then using Ctrl while you unselect any headers or footers, and then making your selection of Stacked or Tabular from the Arrange tab.

But usually I just need this option for a new field I've added.

# Reports: Report Sections

Okay. Now it's time to focus in on just reports because there are a few things you can do with a report that you can't do with a form. Namely, grouping, sorting, and totals. But before we dig into those, we need to discuss the different sections that are available in a report.

## Report Header

The report header appears at the very beginning of your report and will not repeat onto other pages if the report is more than one page long. This is where you can provide the title of the report, your company logo, etc.

You can place a summary field in the report header. If you do so, the summed value will be for the entire report.

Keep in mind that the report header is in addition to the page header, so on the first page of your report you will see them both.

## Page Header

The page header appears at the top of every single page of your report. This is a good place for column labels, for example. Or where you would put your page numbering if you had your page numbering at the top of your report. Access also suggests repeating the name of the report in the page header.

# Group Header

If you choose to group your data within your report, then the group header is what will show at the top of each grouping of your data. Keep in mind that what will show are the different values within your chosen group.

So, if, for example, I group my data on Series Name, then the name of each of my series will be shown in my group header before the report lists detailed information for that group.

You can have a calculated value in your group header. If you do, the calculated value will be for that group and that group only.

You can also have multiple group headers in a report. For example, I have a report that shows profit and loss where the high-level grouping is for type of book (non-fiction, mystery, etc.) and then below that I have another grouping for each category within that type. So my Non-Fiction grouping has categories below that for Computers, Business/Compliance, Budgeting, etc.

When you have multiple groupings, you can have multiple summaries. So, for example, I can have one overall summary for profit and loss for all of my non-fiction titles and then another summary for just those related to computers.

# Detail

Detail is where the most granular level of information is displayed. In the report I mentioned above I have groupings for non-fiction as well as each type of non-fiction, and then under each type of non-fiction, for example, Computers, I have listed each series name (Excel Essentials, Word Essentials, etc.) and information related to units sold, revenue, ad cost, production cost, and profit/loss for each of those series.

I could have just as easily had my detail section be each title that is related to computers instead of each series. What you choose to put in the detail section is up to you and what you want your report to do.

# Group Footer

The group footer is much like the group header except it comes at the end of the group's detail data. This is generally where I include my summary values rather than in the header. As above, you can have as many group footers as there are groupings of your data. Any summary value will be for that grouping level.

# Page Footer

The page footer is what's displayed at the bottom of every single page of your report. This is usually where I have my page numbering. You could also have any copyright notice or other disclaimer you felt needed to be on each page.

# Report Footer

The report footer is only shown on the last page. This is where you can put a total value for the entire report, for example. Any summary value in the report footer will sum values for all groups in the report.

If you look in Design View the report footer shows after the page footer, but that's just in Design View. When the report is actually viewed in Report View or printed, the page footer will be the last thing on the last page and the report footer will come at the end of your data somewhere in the main portion of the page.

Here is the Design View for a report I use of Lifetime Profit and Loss By Genre with Category Detail that gives you a good view of the different sections.

This is a report derived from a query that contains all of the information necessary to generate the report.

Here is the first section of the report (with actual results grayed out), but I wanted you to see the structure this creates.

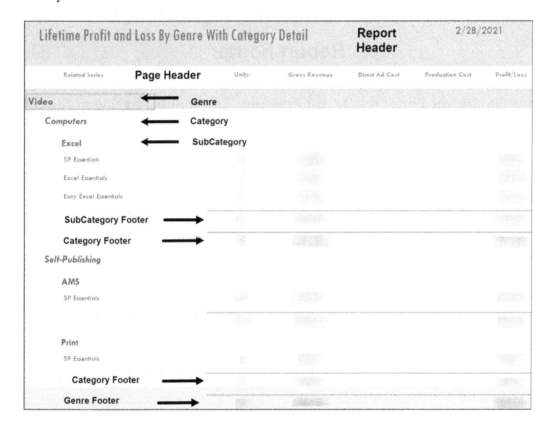

You can see that the Report Header in this report is the report name and the date it was printed. That only appears on the first page.

Next is the Page Header which shows the columns names for the data in the Detail section. (If I were to move those column names down, then they would repeat at each grouping level they'd been moved to. As it's set now they just show at the top of each printed page. I did this because there would have been a lot of repeating information since I would've had to move it to the SubCategory section to really make it work.)

After that is my first Group Header. As you can see in the Design View, Access names each group for the field being used to create the group. In this case it shows as my Genre Header. This is where I list the genre/type of book. For example, Non-Fiction or Mystery or, in this case, Video.

Right after that is another Group Header. This one for Category. These are for the subsets within that genre/type. For example, Computers for Video or Cozy for Mystery.

Next I have another Group Header, this one for SubCategory such as Excel for Computers.

And then we have the Detail section. That's where all of the actual detailed data is shown. In this case I'm showing results by related series, and providing units, revenue, ad cost, production cost, and profit/loss for each series.

After that is the first Group Footer, this one for SubCategory. If you look in Design View, you can see that we're taking the sum of the values from the detail section for each subcategory.

If there was only one series listed in the Detail section, then this just repeats that information. (For example, that happens with Self-Publishing/AMS.)

But if there is more than one series listed, then this row will have the totals of each row in that detail section. For example, that happens with Computers/Excel.)

Below that is the Category footer which sums up the values from all of the SubCategories related to that category. If there was only one subcategory (like for Computers/Excel) then it just repeats the same information from the Subcategory footer.

But if there is more than one subcategory (like for Self-Publishing that has both AMS and Print) then that category footer is the sum of all of the values from the subcategories.

You can also see a genre footer which is the sum of all of the categories under that genre, so in this case the last line is the totals for all Video sales.

Here is that same information but now sorted so that it's at the end of the report to show you how the page numbering and report footers appear as well:

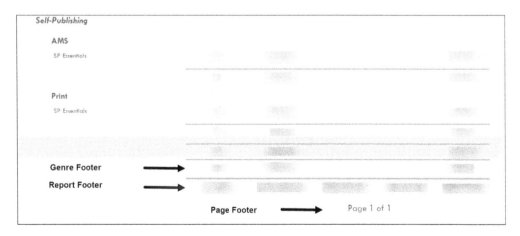

You can see that the very last line of numbers in the report is the Report Footer which includes summary values for all genres in the report. And that below that is the Page Footer which includes the page number.

(Because we're not in print preview this is all one long page so it says Page 1 of 1, but in reality this is Page 8 of 8.)

If you look again at the Design View above, you can see how the structure is sort of a sandwich moving from highest-level to most detailed level and then back out again.

One more thing, you don't have to have headers and footers for each section. In this report I wanted those summary values at each level so I included footers for each level, but I could've skipped that and just had Genre/Category/SubCategory headers with detail and then summary of the detail underneath.

It really comes down to what information you need and what you can display without making it too confusing. Sometimes that's a delicate balancing act.

Another nice thing to know about the different sections of the report is that as you group or total your data, these sections tend to be added for you so you don't have to try to create them yourself. You just have to understand how they work so that you can make edits where you need to.

Okay. So let's talk about Grouping, Sorting, and Totaling your data now.

# Reports: Group Your Data

I'd say at least half of the reports I use have my data grouped on at least one level and sometimes more than one level. For example, I have a report of Profit and Loss By Author with Series Detail. That one has one level of grouping by each author name. But I could as easily have it show title-level detail, too, and group at the series level as well.

Grouping is just a nice way to organize and present data.

## Layout View

The easiest way to do this is probably in Layout View.

Open the report that you want to add a grouping level to in Layout View.

Right-click on the label for the field you want to use for your grouping, and choose "Group On [Field Name]" from the dropdown.

This will move that field to the left-hand side and you'll see that your report is now grouped on that field name, like here where I've grouped the report on Store.

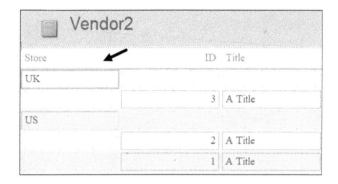

That's one way to group your fields.

Another is to open your report in Layout View and then click on Group & Sort in the Grouping & Totals section of the Design tab. This will make the Group, Sort, and Total section visible below your report.

Click on Add a Group and then choose the field you want to group on from the dropdown menu.

Above you can see where I'd already added the group by Store command.

To add another level of grouping, just do the same thing again. Here's what the report looks like when I'm grouping on Store first and then Author:

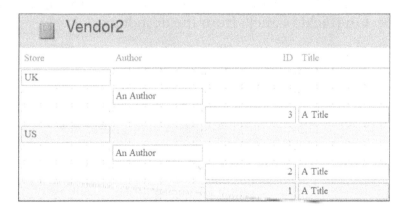

When you have multiple levels of grouping, each subsequent grouping level is made within the prior grouping levels. So here I have two stores, UK and US, and then within each of those it will group by Author name. Since there's only one author, it's one line per grouping.

If I reverse that grouping order so that I group by Author and then Store, there's only one group for Author and one for Store because Store is being grouped under the Author name and in this example I only have one author. Like so:

| Author | Store | | ID | Title |
|--------|-------|--|-----|-------|
| An Author | | | | |
| | UK | | | |
| | | | 3 | A Title |
| | US | | | |
| | | | 2 | A Title |
| | | | 1 | A Title |

Vendor2

If your report is currently grouped on Field A and then Field B and you want to reverse that so that you group on Field B first, you can click on one of the options to highlight it and then use the up and down arrows on the right-hand side of the workspace to change which grouping is performed first.

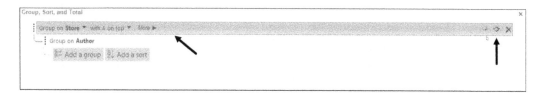

If you start to add a new grouping and change your mind, the X on the right-hand side of the workspace will let you delete that row. It can also be used to delete a grouping (or sort) that you currently have in place for the report.

Each grouping comes with a default sort order as well as other default choices. You can see all of them by clicking on More in the Group, Sort, and Total section. Like so:

Each one can be changed by clicking on the arrows to see the available options in a dropdown menu. The one I usually need to edit is the "do not keep together on one page" option at the end. I like to change this option so that I can keep the header and the first record of each group on the same page.

# Design View

You can also group your records in Design View.

To do so, open your report in Design View. Right-click on the field you want to group on, and choose Group On from the dropdown menu.

Your results will be grouped by that field and you will now have a Group Header section for that group, but there will be no fields in the header section. The data will just have spaces between each grouping but the actual values for the group you chose will remain in the detail section like in this example where I've chosen to group on Author:

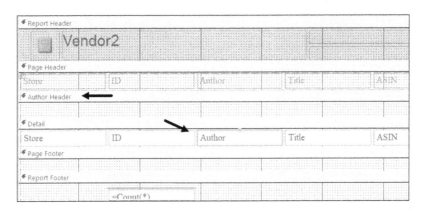

You can cut and paste the text box for that field from the Details section to the Group Header section if you want the value to be shown in the title header section but not in the detail section. (If you do so, be sure to also delete the associate label text box from the Page Header section.) To paste, click on the group header name (in this case Author Header) and then paste and the field should then appear in the group header field section.

If you want the text in both the detail section and the group header section, you can add a new text box into the Group Header section using the Controls options under the Design tab.

Click on the Text Box option, which is the second one. Go to the header section and click and drag to create a text box. (Up and over or down and over or over and down, etc.)

Type into that text box, which for me shows as Unbound, the field name for the field you're grouping on. In this case Author.

Then delete the associated label box that Access created at the same time which for me for this example was showing the text Text 110. It will be different for you.

That will look something like this in your report:

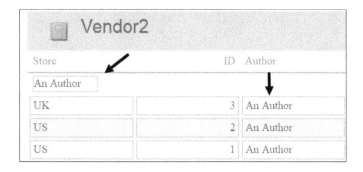

The Group, Sort, and Total section in Design View works generally the same way as it does in Layout View. You can add a grouping from there, too, but it will have that same Design View issue where there is no field in the group header section.

# Reports: Sort Your Data

As we've touched on a bit above, you can also sort your report by any of your data fields.

## Group, Sort, and Totals Section

The easiest way to do this is go to Design or Layout View and pull up the Group, Sort, and Totals section if it isn't already visible, and then click on Add a Sort or change the sort for an already grouped or sorted field.

To sort a new field when you click on Add a Sort you'll be given a list of field names to choose from. Select the one you want to sort on. The default will be to sort in ascending order (from A to Z, from smallest to largest, etc.), but you can click on that arrow for that option and change it to sort in descending order instead.

You can also choose how many characters to sort on for text or to sort on an interval for numbers. The default is to sort on the entire value.

You can add more than one level of sorting to your report, just keep in mind that the first level will always be the dominant sort order. So if I, for example, sort by ID there's no point in sorting on anything else because my ID field is unique.

Also note that for sorts there's nothing in your report that will indicate the sort order you're using. You can usually identify it visually.

## Layout View

In Layout View you can right-click on a field you want to sort by and choose your sort option. For example, Sort A to Z or Sort Z to A.

Both the ascending and descending options for that field type will be available to choose from.

When you do add a sort this way it will also appear in the Group, Sort, and Totals section down below.

This option only works if you want to sort by one field, not multiple fields. When I tried to add a second field to the sort by right-clicking on a different field and choosing a sort order, it overwrote the sort for the first one.

## Design View

In Design View you can also right-click on a field you want to sort by and choose your sort option from the dropdown menu, but again it only works if you want to sort by one field. Your sort will also appear in the Group, Sort, and Totals section.

* * *

If you're both grouping and sorting your data, pay attention to the order in which you group and sort. If you have, for example, a sort on units before you have a grouping on author name, then the sort on the number of units will take precedence over the grouping on author name making the grouping probably useless. But if you put the grouping first then the data would group on author name and sort on units only after that had happened.

Remember, you can use the up and down arrows in the Group, Sort, and Total workspace to change the order of your groups and sorts.

Also, in case you run into this issue, if you ever try to sort on a summed value that you've added to your report, that isn't possible using the sorting options as we've just walked through them. You'd need to have those sums in the query or table that you pull from for the report to sort on them.

# Reports: Add Summary Values

Speaking of sums, let's talk about how you add totals to your report.

I like to get all my groups in order first. Once you have that, it's pretty straight-forward.

## Layout View

Click onto the label for the field where you want to add a totals value. Then go to the Grouping & Totals section of the Design tab, click on the dropdown arrow next to Totals, and choose the summary type you want to use.

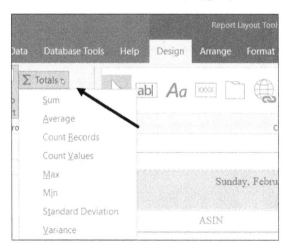

I almost exclusively use Sum, but your other options are Average, Count Records, Count Values, Max, Min, Standard Deviation, and Variance.

That will add a calculation at each level of your report.

You can also right-click on the field name to bring up the dropdown menu, then go to Total [Field Name], and then choose your summation option from the secondary dropdown menu.

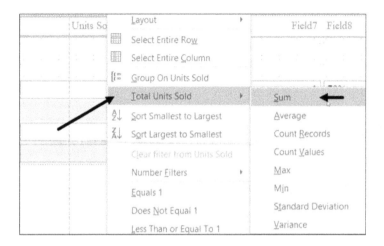

(Just a word of warning that if you're going to mix and match these and have a sum for one and a count for another, for example, you really need to find a way to properly label those results so it's clear what summation value is being provided for each field.)

Also, if you don't group first, Access will not automatically add summary values for the any new grouping levels you later add.

## Design View

In Design View, you can click onto either the label text box or the data text box for the field you want to summarize and then click on your choice from the Totals dropdown in the Grouping & Totals section of the Design tab.

Like above, if your data has already been grouped, this will add a summary field at every level even if that means adding in footers that didn't previously exist for those levels.

And, just like above, if you add your totals first and then group, they will not carry through to your new group levels.

You can also right-click on the field you want to total, go to Total in the dropdown menu, and then choose your totals option in the secondary dropdown. Note that in this case the option in the dropdown menu just says Total and doesn't include the field name, too, like it does in Layout View.

# Group, Sort, and Total

If you have groups or sorts listed in the Group, Sort, and Total section, you can also go into the More options for that group or sort and change the fourth option to say which field you want to count or sum related to that group or sort.

With the checkboxes, this option gives you more control over which level to summarize at. You can check and uncheck the boxes to see the various options in play in your report.

If under that grouping you want more than one field to be summarized, you need to add each field separately.

\* \* \*

By default Access is going to use a gridline with your different totals fields so they'll have a dark gray line above them.

I usually also change the font, or use bold or italics for the field to further distinguish it from my detail numbers. And I also sometimes add a little extra space in Design View for the totals values to set them apart from my main data.

Finally, I often find that the totals text boxes need to be resized to effectively show their values. They're generally too short for some reason.

# Reports: Conditional Formatting

Conditional formatting lets you add bolding, italics, underline, a different font color, or a different fill color to a text box if certain criteria are met.

I hadn't really used this in the past, but after I wrote the original *Intermediate Access* I started using it a lot.

If you're already familiar with how this works in Excel, it's very straight-forward.

In either Layout View or Design View, click into the data portion of the field where you want to have your conditional formatting applied. (So in Layout View, click on one of the entries. In Design View click on the data text box for that field.)

You'll know you've done this correctly when you go to the Format tab and under the Control Formatting section the Conditional Formatting option is available to you and not grayed out.

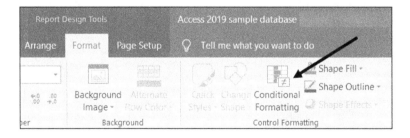

Click on it to bring up the Conditional Formatting Rules Manager dialogue box. You can also right-click in your cell and choose Conditional Formatting from the dropdown menu. Either way, this is what you'll see:

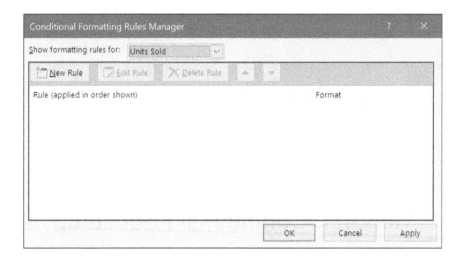

Click on New Rule to add a new rule. If you already have rules in place you'll also be able to click on Edit Rule and Delete Rule.

You have two choices, "check values in the current record or use an expression" or "compare to other records".

To build a simple rule that formats values greater than a set amount, keep the first option (check values) selected, and then set your criteria and your formatting in the section down below that, like here where I've set it so that any units sold value greater than 5 will be highlighted green.

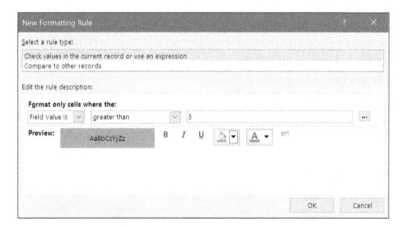

Rather than add a set value you can also click on the ... and add an expression that is built off of fields in your database.

The compare to other records option allows you to add data bars to your report to visually flag your records. You can do so for lowest to highest value, absolute values, or based on percentages. (Top 10%, etc.)

Here is one where I let it use the default color and create data bars for lowest to highest values:

| Date of Sale | Title | Publisher | Units Sold |
|---|---|---|---|
| 8/1/2017 | A Title | An Author | 1 |
| 8/2/2017 | A Title | An Author | 2 |
| 8/3/2017 | A Title Revised | An Author | 4 |
| 8/6/2017 | A Title Revised | An Author | 1 |
| 8/10/2017 | A Title | An Author | 1 |
| 8/1/2017 | Another Title | An Author | 6 |
| 8/2/2017 | A Third Title | An Author | 1 |
| 8/3/2017 | A Title | An Author | 3 |
| 8/6/2017 | Another Title | An Author | 1 |
| 8/10/2017 | Another Title | An Author | 5 |
| 8/1/2017 | Another Title | An Author | 1 |
| 8/2/2017 | Another Title | An Author | 9 |
| 8/3/2017 | Another Title | An Author | 1 |
| 8/6/2017 | A Third Title | An Author | 11 |
| 8/10/2017 | A Third Title | An Author | 1 |

You can see that when the units were the largest value, 11, that the data bar was the longest. And when the units were the lowest value, 1, the data bar was the shortest.

When you've made all of your selections, click OK, and then click OK again to go back to your report.

You can go back in to edit or delete an existing rule the same way you went in to create a new one, just be sure that you have the correct field selected when looking for an existing rule. If you don't, you can always change the field name in the dropdown menu at the top of the Conditional Formatting Rules Manager dialogue box.

To edit or delete a rule, click on the rule and then choose Edit Rule or Delete Rule.

You can have more than one rule apply to a field. The order in which they appear will dictate which rule is applied first. The order can be the difference between a rule working and not, so if a rule you create doesn't seem to be running, check for rule order.

**M.L. Humphrey**

Also, I was able to apply the check values formatting option to a summary field by clicking on the summary field before I built the rule, but I wasn't able to apply the compare to other records option. Access acted like it would work, but then didn't show the data bars I'd supposedly added.

# Print Preview

I've touched on this before, but this is a good time to remind you that you should always print preview documents that you want to print from Access. I have had far too many times when a form or report looked horrible in printed form to not do this each and every time.

Reports have Print Preview built in as a View option. So you can just go to View in the Design or Home tab and select Print Preview from there. Or right-click in the workspace and choose Print Preview from the dropdown menu.

Forms do not have Print Preview built in as a View option so you need to go to the File tab, choose Print on the left-hand side, and then choose Print Preview that way.

Whichever way you get there it will then show you a preview of your form or report as it will print. You will also have options under the Page Size and Page Layout sections of the Print Preview tab to change your page size, margins, and page orientation (portrait or landscape).

(The Zoom section options just let you change how the print preview shows in your workspace. The Data section options allow you to export the document rather than print it.)

The arrows at the bottom of the print preview workspace let you move through the document one printed page at a time.

Always, always check for fields that continue on to the next page so you can go back and fix those.

Also, remember that narrowing your margins or changing the orientation may easily fix a form or report that carries over onto a second page.

To print a document double-sided, you need to choose to Print and then click on Properties in the Print dialogue box. Usually if you make that choice once it will save for the next time you choose to print that particular document.

# Other Tips and Tricks

A few more random tidbits to share with you:

## Refresh Data

I often find myself working back and forth between a few data tables and a query or report to get the query or report working properly. Sometimes this requires making an update to my data. (For example, to list an identifier in my master table that was missing.)

When I have a query or report already open and I make an update like that to a data table that is feeding into the query or report, the query or report does not automatically update. To get it to update I need to use the Refresh All option in the Records section of the Home tab. This refreshes the data in your query or report without you having to close it and reopen it.

If you still have the data table open, sometimes the refresh won't work. So be sure to close the data table before you Refresh All. (Usually when this happens to me I'm pretty sure it's because I'm still clicked into the field where I made the update so it really hasn't been recorded yet.)

## Compact & Repair

I'll admit, I don't do this probably near as much as I should, but you should periodically compact and repair your database. It will clean up space that's being used that doesn't need to be and may improve performance.

To do this, go to the File tab, then click on Info, and then choose Compact & Repair.

When I did this on the database I was using to write the original Access books, it was 2 MB before I ran it and 1 MB after. So doing so halved the size of my database. I also just did it to my database I use for tracking sales where I'd gone through and changed some field names and it went from 32 MB to 10 MB.

So if size or performance is an issue, well worth doing. But if your database contains original data or is in some other way irreplaceable, save a backup copy first.

You can also Compact & Repair from the Database Tools tab under the Tools section.

## Export to PDF

If you want to send a report from Access to another user via email, exporting that report to a PDF file is probably an easy way to do so.

To export a report (or table or query or form) to a PDF, select it, go to the External Data tab, and choose PDF or XPS under the Export section. This will bring up a Publish as PDF or XPS dialogue box. Choose where you want it to save, rename it if you need to, and then click on Publish.

Keep in mind that the document you generate in PDF format will have the same issues that you'd have in printing from Access, which is why I would generally only use this for a well-formatted form or report that has already been checked in Print Preview.

I do now generate my monthly reports as PDFs rather than print them because I went through a period where my printer would get stuck every time I printed a document and it was so annoying I just started working in PDFs instead. It's just as easy as printing a document, really. (Easier in my case.)

## Find

Access does have a find and a replace function just like in other Office programs. I'd be very leery of using the replace portion of it given the way changes to data stick in Access, but Find can be a handy way for locating a specific record.

You have a couple options here.

You can open your table, query, form, or report and then click on the Find option in the Find section of the Home tab. This will bring up the Find dialogue box for reports or queries or the Find and Replace dialogue box for tables and forms.

Type in what you want to find in the Find What field on the Find tab and then choose where you want to look. If you just want to look in a specific field you need to be clicked into it before you open the dialogue box.

It appears from my testing that Find will only work on detailed data entries. It doesn't seem to work on group headings or labels. This can be particularly useful to know if you are building a large report and wanted to search on a field that you're making into a group header. In that case you may want to duplicate your data and leave that value in a column in the detail section as well.

You can also use Ctrl + F to bring up the Find or the Find and Replace dialogue box.

# AutoCorrect

I've yet to run into this because for the most part I upload my data into Access rather than adding new entries directly in Access, but it turns out that Access has an AutoCorrect feature which will change your data entries on you.

If you immediately notice that it's done so, you can use Ctrl + Z to change the entry back. But it's probably an even better idea if you're using your database for direct entry to turn AutoCorrect off entirely.

To do so, click on the File tab, and then click on Options on the left-hand side. From there click on Proofing and then on the AutoCorrect Options button. Uncheck the box for "Replace Text as You Type" to turn off all AutoCorrect. And then click OK and OK again.

# Change Navigation Pane Options

One last tip. This is something I've never needed, but I did accidentally trigger it at one point and I could see how it might be useful under certain circumstances.

What I call the All Access Objects pane is what Access calls the Navigation Pane. This is the pane that is on the left-hand side of the screen. It can be minimized, but it can't be closed.

By default it shows all of your tables, queries, forms, and reports in that order with the objects in each category then listed alphabetically.

But it turns out you can change this.

If you left-click on the gray arrow next to All Access Objects you will see a dropdown menu of choices:

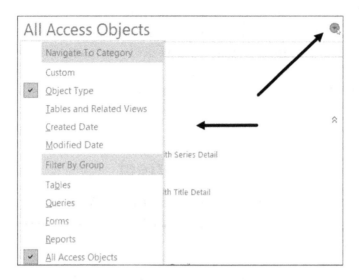

The Tables and Related Views choice will rearrange the pane so that each table is shown with its associated queries, forms, and reports listed underneath.

The Created Date option will group your objects by when they were created. The database I've been using for these books shows with Last Week, Two Weeks Ago, and Older as the categories. So this is probably an easy way to see what has been added to a database recently.

The Modified Date option will group your objects by when they were last modified. My categories for this one are showing the days of this week from Sunday onward, Last Week, Two Weeks Ago, and Older. So a good way to check what tables, queries, forms, or reports have been recently modified especially in a shared database.

Below those choices is a grayed in header that reads Filter By Group. And below that are the groupings available for your given selection.

For example, with Object Type as the view I have Tables, Queries, Forms, Reports, and All Access Objects listed there.

I could click on Tables, Queries, Forms, or Reports to show files that are only that category type.

With Tables and Related Views chosen, it lists the individual table names.

So something to play around with, but not something I've ever needed to use myself.

# Where To Go From Here

Alright, so that's all we're going to cover here.

There are still things that I haven't covered about Access. My goal with these books was to provide you the information I think you need but in manageable chunks.

At this point most of what I haven't covered is information I don't think you'll use much. Like how to have a hyperlink field or to use Access to create a web app. Or how to split your Access database when it's a shared database.

And some of the topics are just way more advanced than the average user needs to know, like using macros and Visual Basic.

But you may need to know about one of those topics one day. So how do you find the answers?

Access help is a great place to start. You can click on the Help tab and then on Help again. That will bring up a Help task pane. There is also a Show Training option under Help.

In addition, I think that the Microsoft website is incredibly helpful. I usually get there by doing an internet search and including microsoft in the search terms so that one of my first search results will link to the support.office.com or the microsoft.com websites.

When doing this keep in mind that at the top of every help topic they show which versions of Access the article applies to, like this one called Introduction to Reports in Access:

Introduction to reports in Access

See the line directly below that that lists the various Access iterations it covers.

And, of course, there's a general internet search. Most problems you encounter will not be new ones. Someone out there has tried to figure out how to do the same thing you are and you can search for those questions and answers to find the solution.

Or, if you're brave, you can ask the question yourself on one of the many, many user forums that exist for these types of questions. Just try to be as detailed as possible when doing so about what version of Access you're using.

You can also contact me. Although I'll warn you that since I approach Access as an Excel user rather than a database developer that a lot of what I haven't covered at this point is parts of Access I simply don't use. I can look up an answer for you and provide a link, but if you're trying to implement the table analyzer or the database documenter that's just not something I'll have any experience with personally. But I'll try to help you the best I can.

# Conclusion

Okay. So that's it. At this point you should be able to comfortably work in most basic Access databases or create one yourself as well as generate nice printed reports of your results.

Remember when working in Access (or any Office program) that it has a certain underlying logic to it. Access probably the least of all of the Office programs, but it's still there.

If you know that basic structure you can guess where something will be located or how it might work. Often that's how I figure out things in Excel, Word, PowerPoint, and Access. I think, "This should be possible" and then I go looking where I think it should be in that program.

Because changes in Access can be so permanent, always back things up before you get too involved in making changes. Since everything depends on relationships and the flow of data from tables to queries, forms, and reports, Access is the easiest of the Office programs to break.

If you do make changes to field names or relationships or queries, double-check your existing forms and reports to make sure they're still working.

Keep in mind that an unexpected parameter dialogue box is very likely an indication that a query somewhere along the line isn't pulling in a field that it needs in order to work. (That's for an unexpected parameter dialogue box, not just any parameter dialogue box.)

Access is an incredibly powerful tool. I don't know how I'd track my writing business without it. But do use it with care. Proceed slowly and check and double-check that your results make sense.

Always, always have ways that you can verify that a result is what you expect it to be. This may mean keeping track of values outside of Access, or using filters to verify a data upload worked correctly.

Whatever you do, don't just trust blindly. Always check. Always ask, does this make sense? Is this what I should be seeing?

But don't let it intimidate you either. You can do this. Just slow and steady. You'll get it to work if you take the time and work it through. It's all about logic and relationships.

Alright, then. Good luck with it.

# INDEX

## ABOUT THE AUTHOR

M.L. Humphrey is a former stockbroker with a degree in Economics from Stanford and an MBA from Wharton who has spent close to twenty years as a regulator and consultant in the financial services industry.

————————————

You can reach M.L. at mlhumphreywriter@gmail.com or at mlhumphrey.com.

www.ingramcontent.com/pod-product-compliance
Lightning Source LLC
Chambersburg PA
CBHW080359060326
40689CB00019B/4062